Autophotography

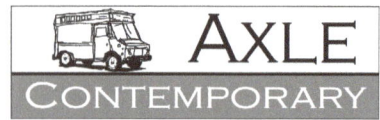

Published by
Axle Contemporary
P.O. Box 22095
Santa Fe, New Mexico 87502

ISBN 978-0-9858116-4-8

www.axlepress.com

Designed by Matthew Chase-Daniel and Jerry Wellman

Cover photograph: Guy Cross, Coming Into Santa Fe, 1978

Autophotography

Self-Portraits by New Mexico Photographers

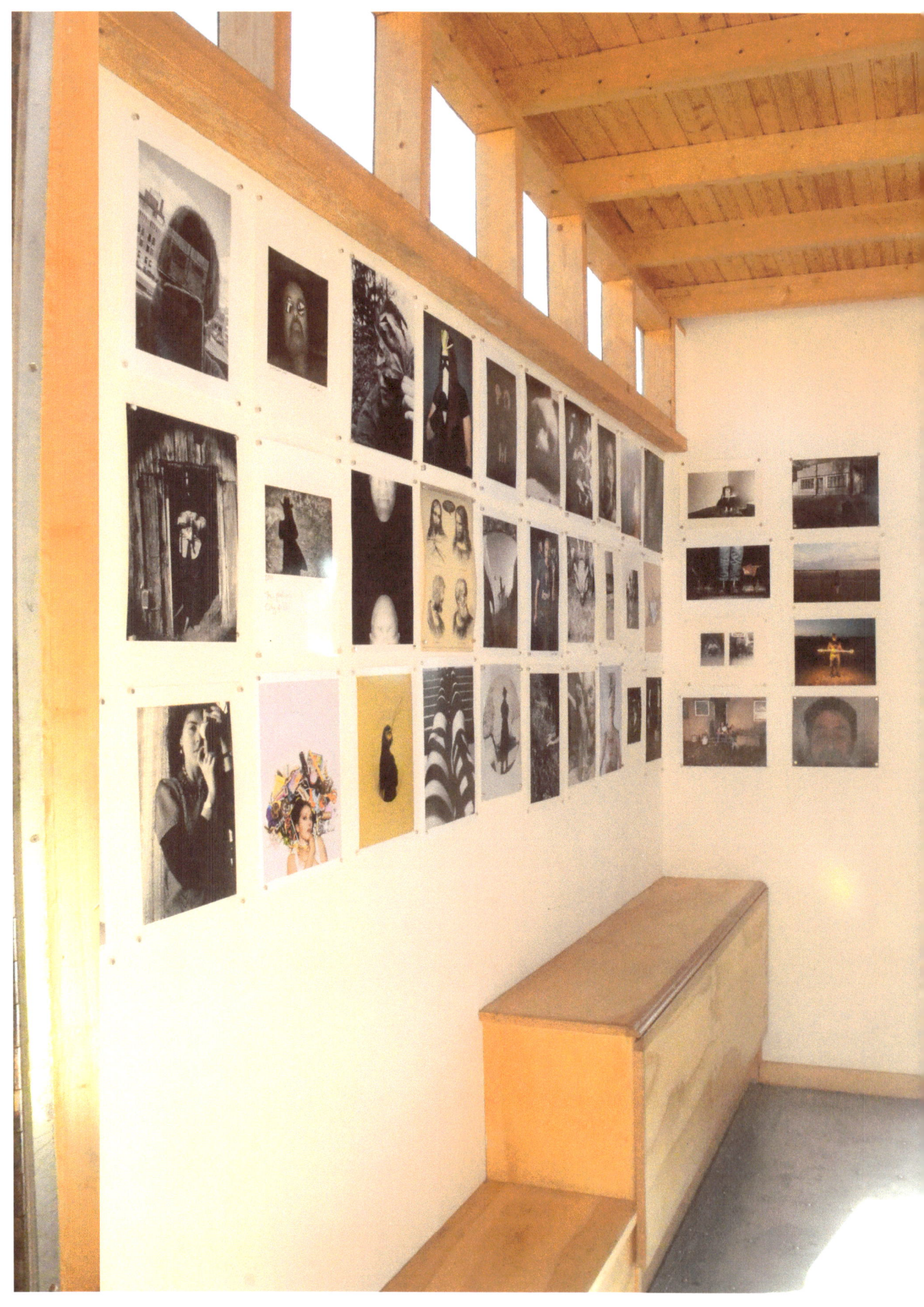

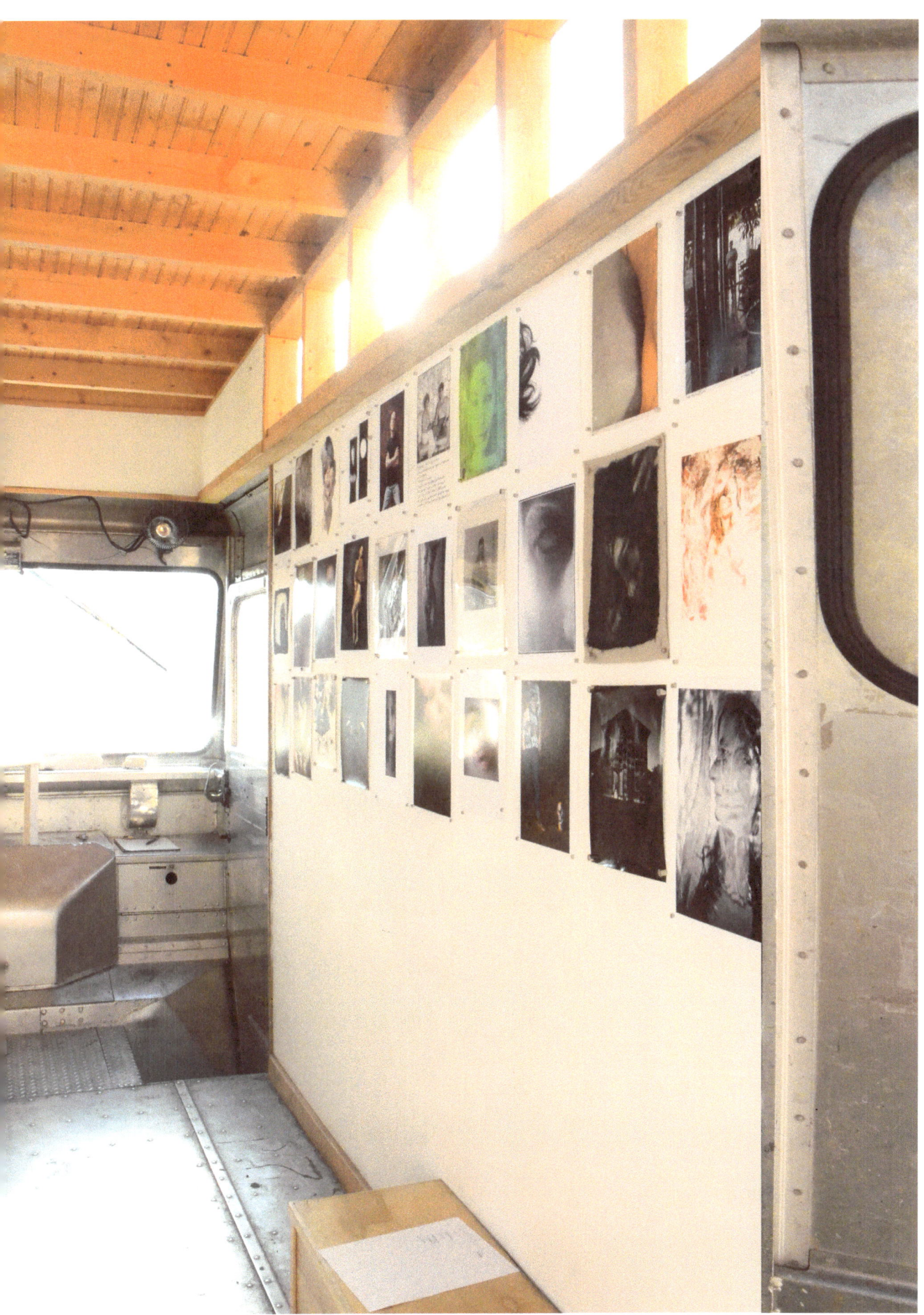

Autophotography, installed at the Axle Contemporary mobile gallery, October, 2013

The Photographers

V. Amore

Henry Aragoncillo

Laurie Archer

Phillip Augustin

Brad Bealmear

Jonathan Blaustein

Gay Block

Iscah Hunsden Carey

Matthew Chase-Daniel

Carola Clift

William Clift

Eric Cosineau

Guy Cross

Ungelbah Davilla

Antone Dolezal

Dianne Duenzl

Jennifer Esperanza

Steve Fitch

Patricia Galagan

Kirk Gittings

Lydia Gonzales

Sondra Goodwin

Meggan Gould

Lauren Greenwald

James Hart

Sol Hill

Megan Jacobs

Jen Judge

David Michael Kennedy

Lisa Law

Willis F. Lee

Louis Leray

Patti Levey

Tamara Lichtenstein

Herbert Lotz

Jessamyn Lovell

Richard Lowenberg

Helen Maringer

Gabriella Marks

Elliott McDowell

Nick Merrick

Philip Metcalf

Lia Moldovan	Frances Seward
Duane Monczewski	Laura Shields
Delilah Montoya	Brandon Soder
Sarah Moore	Catie Soldan
Jonathan Morse	Nancy Sutor
Joseph Mougel	Anne Staveley
Teresa Neptune	Sharon Stewart
Nic Nicosia	Jamey Stillings
Clay Peres	Robert Stivers
Jane Phillips	Dianne Stromberg
Daniel Quat	Jim Stone
Dave Reichert	Martin Stupich
Meridel Rubenstein	Carrie Tafoya
Janet Russek	Laurie Tümer
Kate Russell	Lisa Tyrrell
Ward Russell	Marion Wasserman
Tara Raye Russo	Melanie West
Key Sanders	Will Wilson
Celia Luz Santos	Baron Wolman
Suzanne Sbarge	Francesca Yorke
David Scheinbaum	Joan Zalenski
Jennifer Schlesinger Hanson	Zoë Zimmerman
Andrea Senutovitch	

Photography, still a young art form, has experienced dramatic changes in the last hundred years as the medium has become more and more accessible. In the last decade, these changes have accelerated rapidly with the advent of affordable digital technologies for shooting and printing.

Since the 1800's, New Mexico has provided inspiration to some of the best photographers in the world. Since the 1920's, many great photographers have located here and produced some of the most compelling modern work in the medium. Important works have been produced here by photographers such as Ansel Adams, Paul Strand, Edward Weston, Laura Gilpin, Eliot Porter, Lee Friedlander, Henri Cartier-Bresson, and Robert Frank. In the late 20th and early 21st centuries, dozens of professional photographers have chosen New Mexico as a place to live and work.

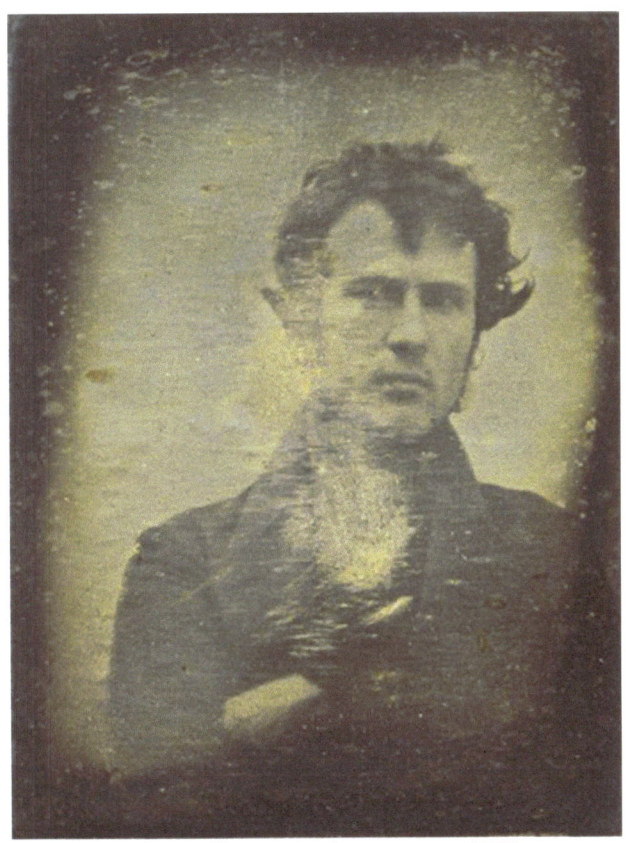

Robert Cornelius, self-portrait, daguerrotype, 1839

Portraiture has been a focus of photography from early on, and self-portraiture has been a part of this since the beginning. One of the first photographic portraits ever created was in fact a self-portrait, by Robert Cornelius. And now the "selfie" has become a staple of youth culture on social media websites.

A self-portrait is not a reflection. With our own eyes, our own focus, it is rare that we actually see ourselves. A minute or two in front of the morning mirror may be all for our day. Even in those brief moments we usually simply look, but we do not see, do not observe. For a self-portrait a unique commitment is necessary. The presentation of self to the world and in the world is consciously engaged. Whatever the technique or concept initially undertaken, the result, an image and a physical object, remains as a small capture of the artist's spirit. In a sense every photograph is a self-portrait. The photograph comes from the sustaining interest of the photographer. It reveals something of the photographer's passion and self.

For Autophotography, Axle Contemporary assembled an exhibition which includes many of the most compelling photographers working now in the state. The participants include photographers known for diverse genres: Landscape, portraiture, architectural, fine art, commercial, fashion, environmental, conceptual, journalism, abstract, and wedding photography. We've invited these artists to exhibit works of self-portraiture. Process ranges from 8x10 view cameras to smartphone photos, from split-toned waxed callotype to digitally manipulated inkjet prints, collage, and monoprinting. For many of the artists, this exhibition has provided an opportunity for experimentation and reflection, outside of the artist's established oeuvre. We are pleased to share this rich portrait of a community of artist-photographers working in New Mexico at this time, by the photographers themselves.

Matthew Chase-Daniel and Jerry Wellman
Axle Contemporary
Santa Fe, 2013

V. Amore

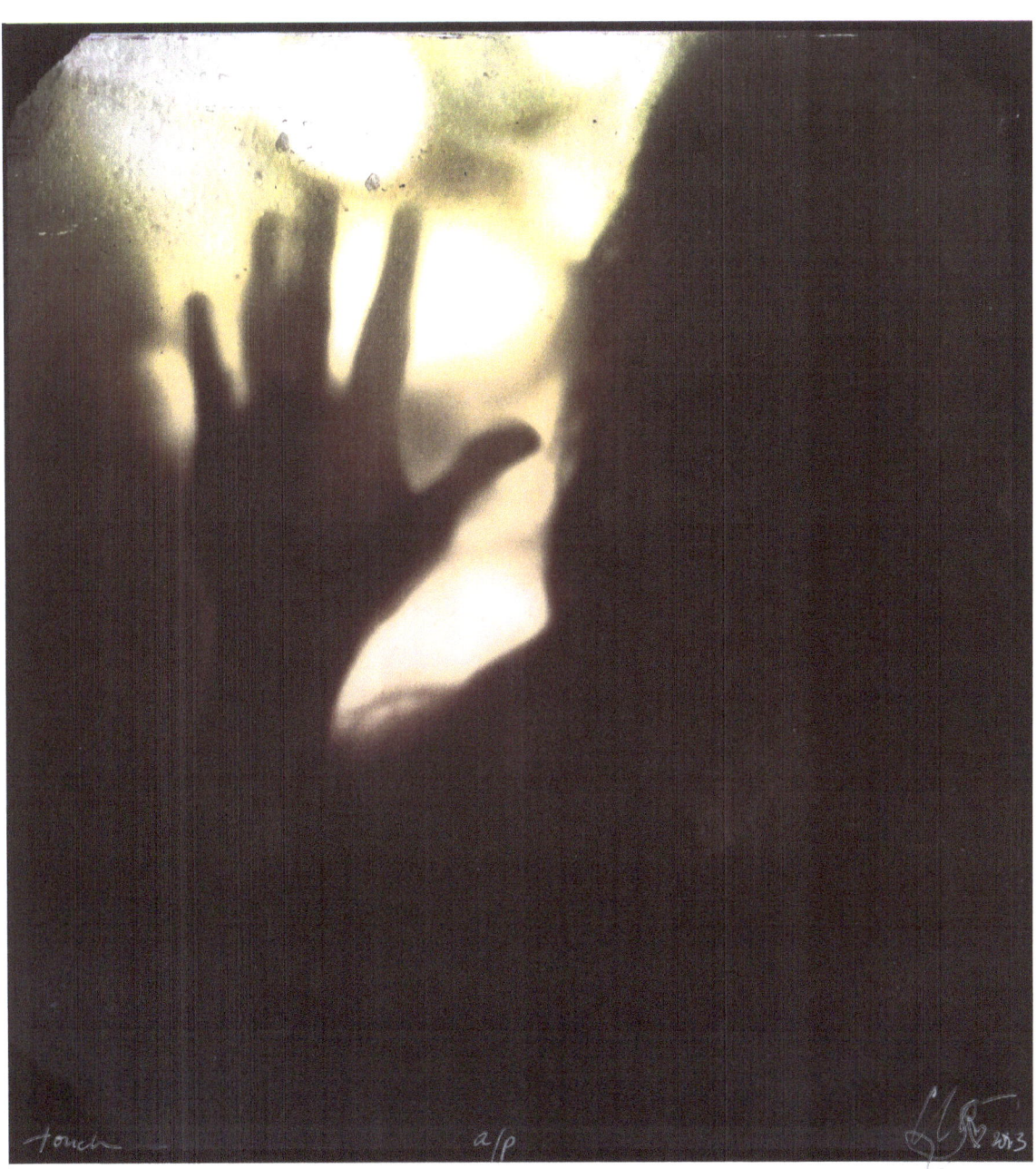

touch　　　　　　　　　　　　　　a/p

Henry Aragoncillo

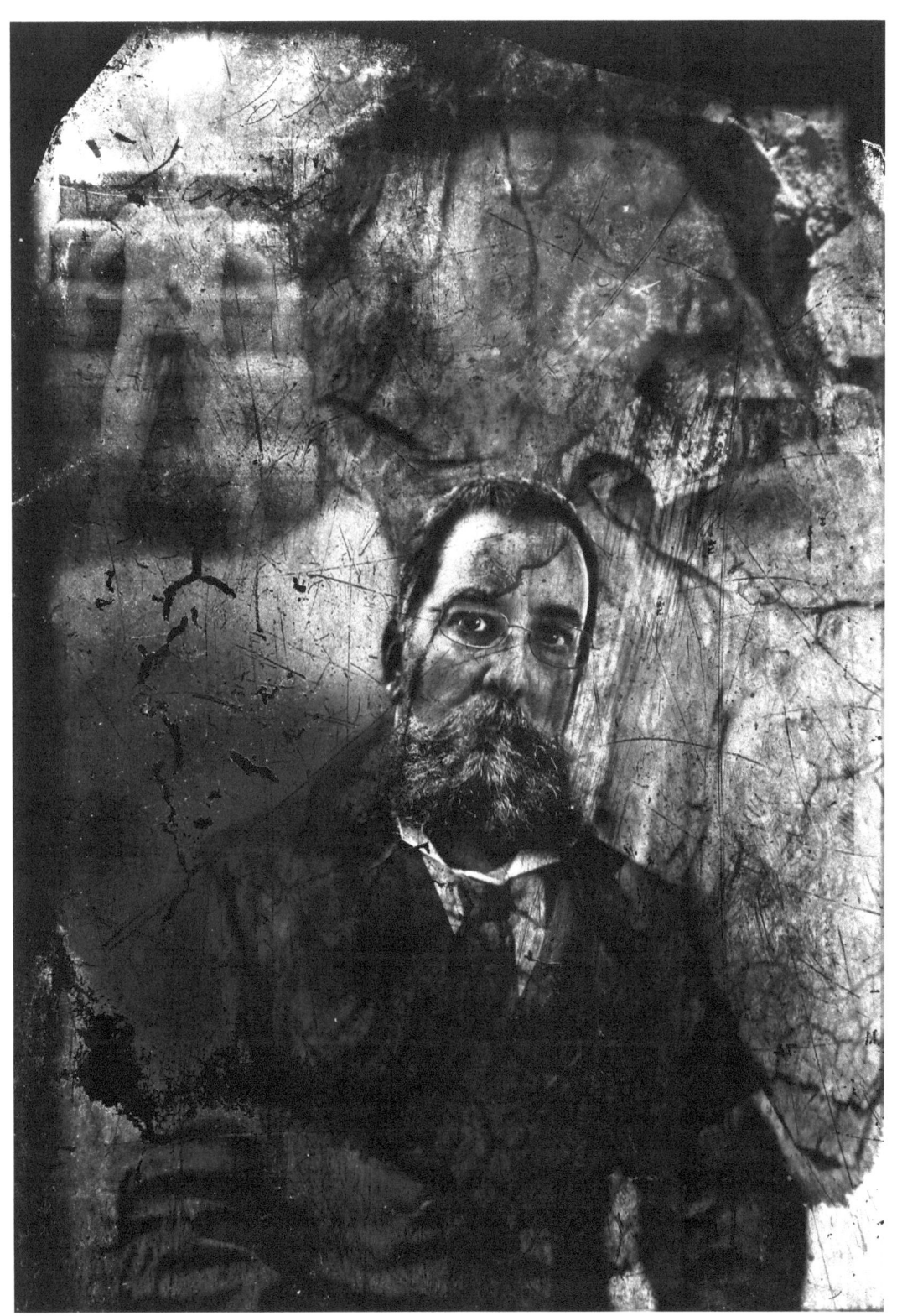

Laurie Archer

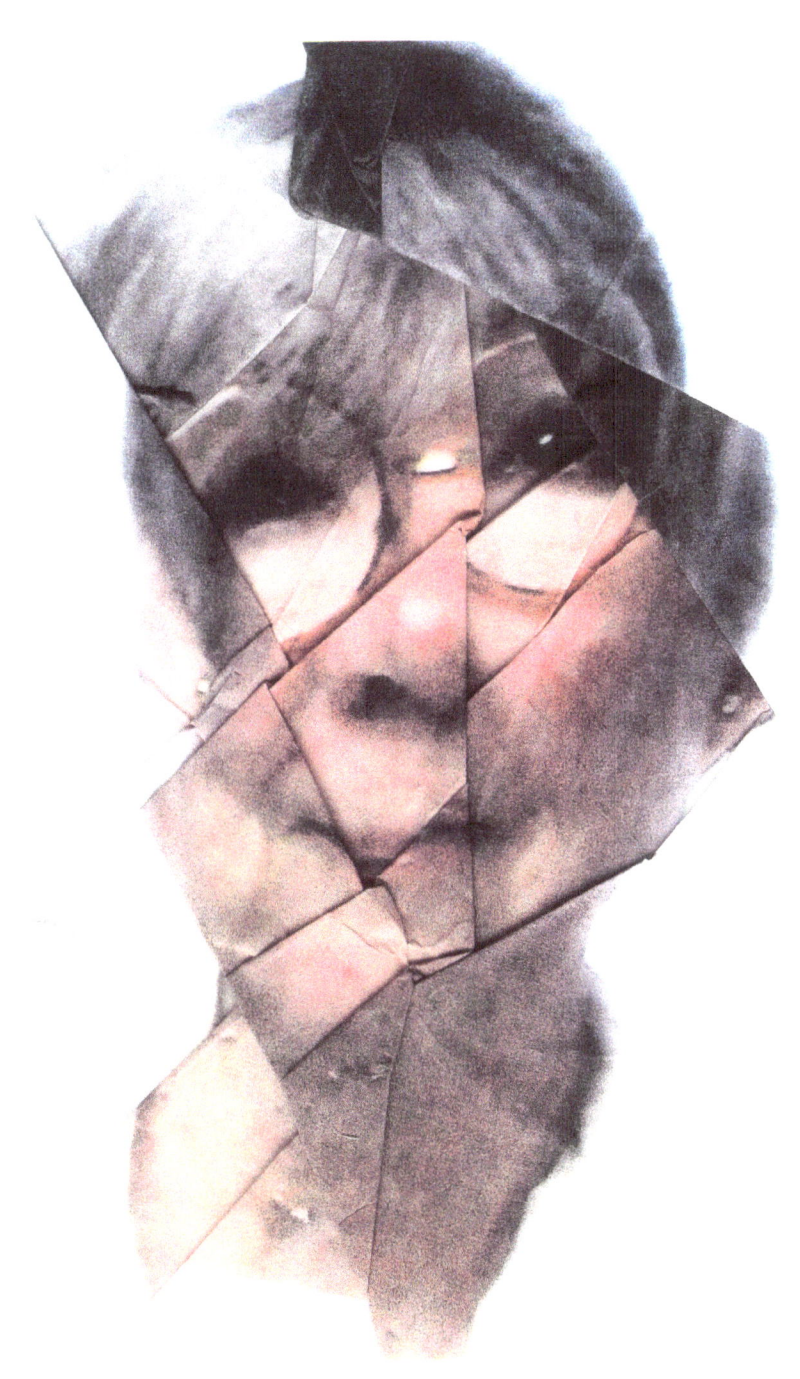

Phillip Augustin

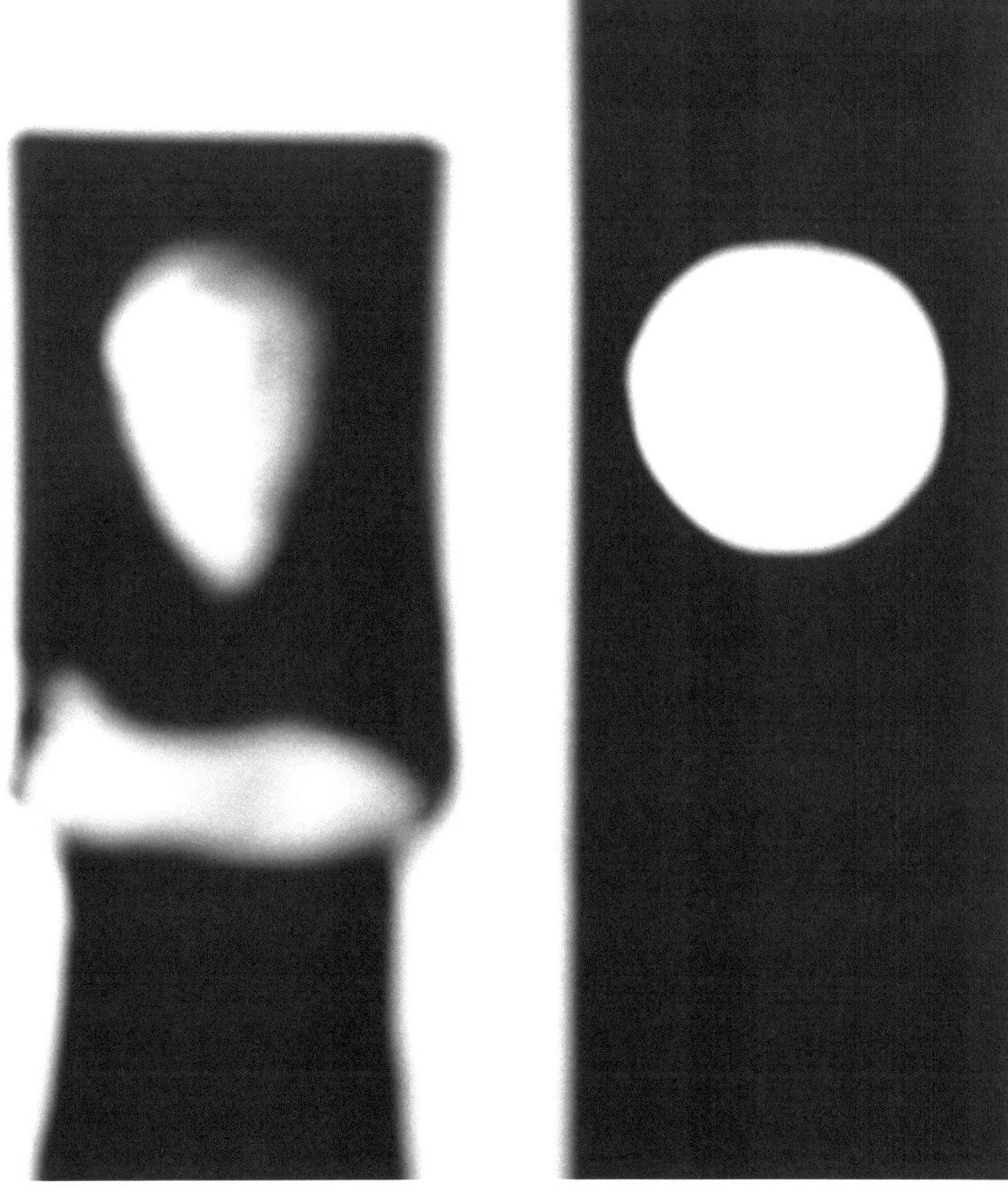

Brad Bealmear

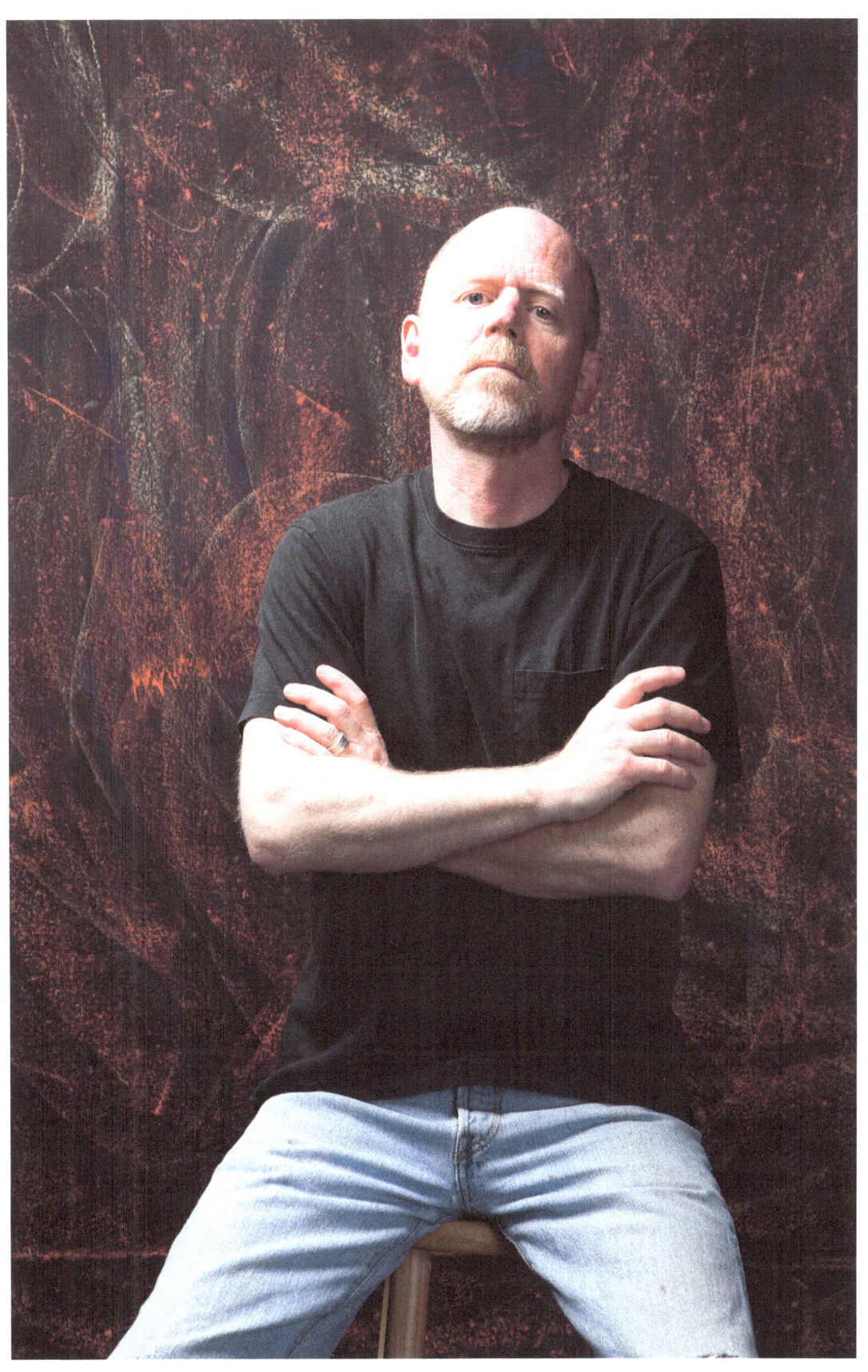

Jonathan Blaustein

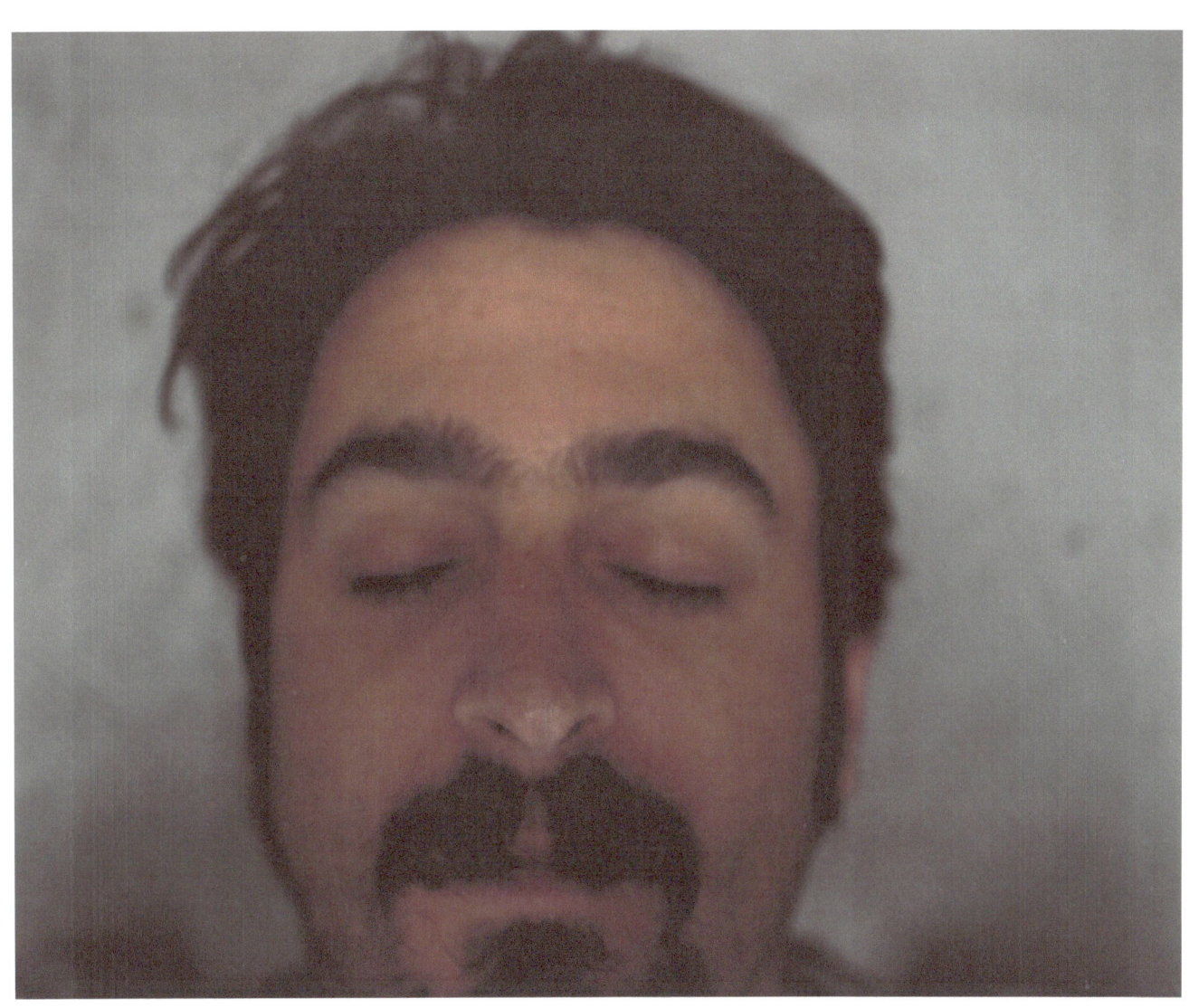

Gay Block

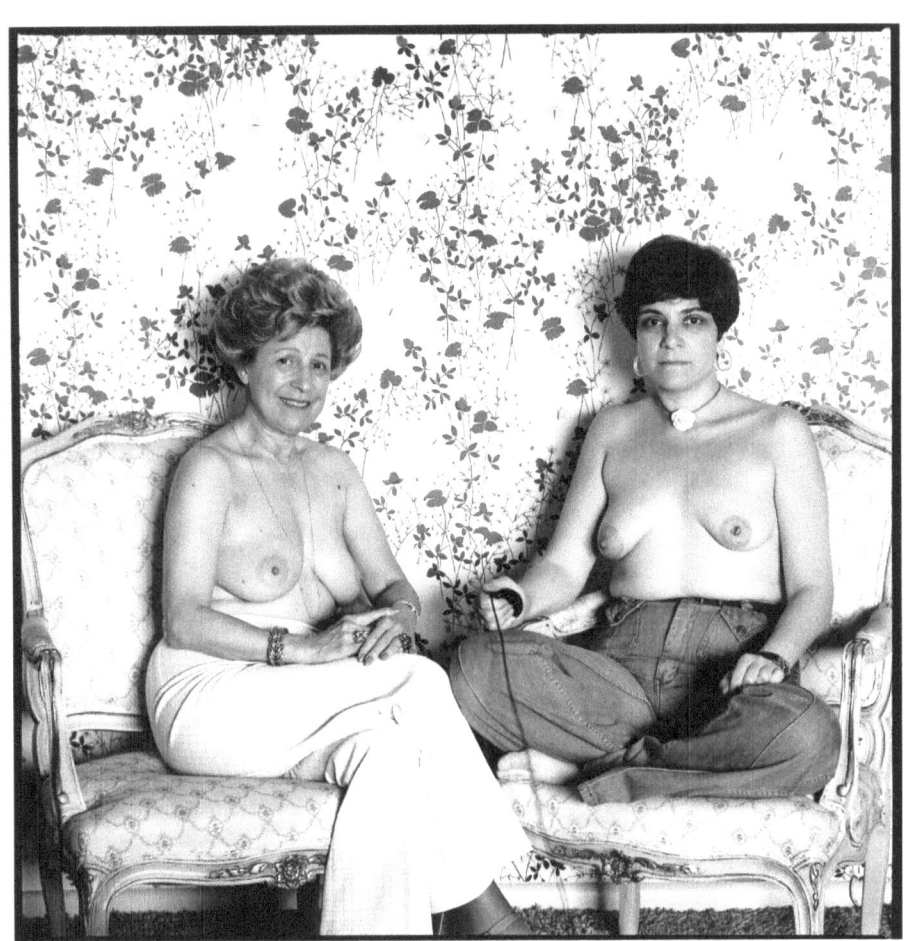

"Hi darling. This is a nice surprise!"
"I was in the neighborhood and thought we'd take some
pictures together."
"That would be lovely."
I suggest we pose bare-breasted. You like the idea.
Then you say it. Again. I knew you would.
"It's too bad your breasts aren't as pretty as mine."
Two years later you allow me to exhibit this image
in Houston. What do your friends say? My children don't like it.

Iscah Hunsden Carey

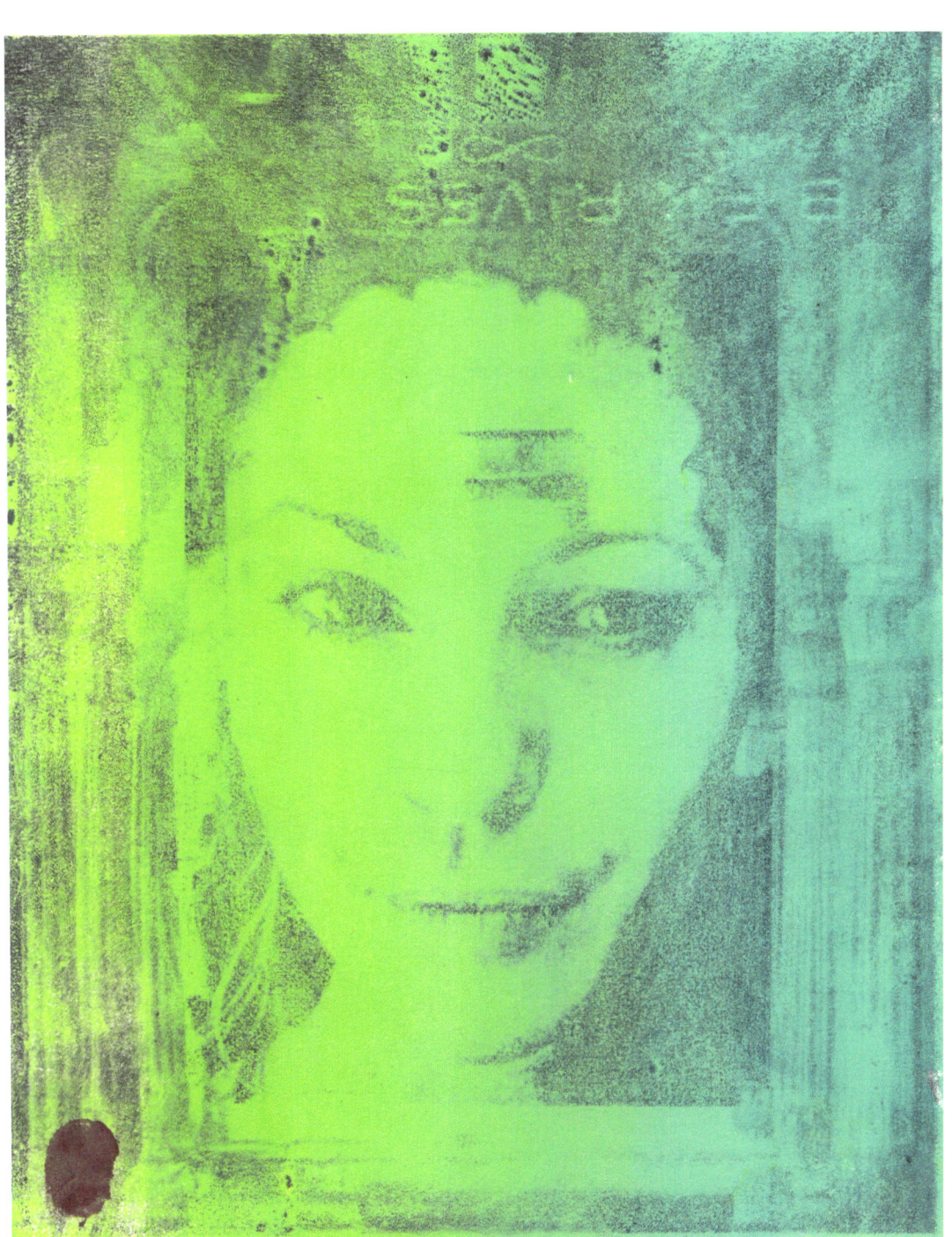

Matthew Chase-Daniel

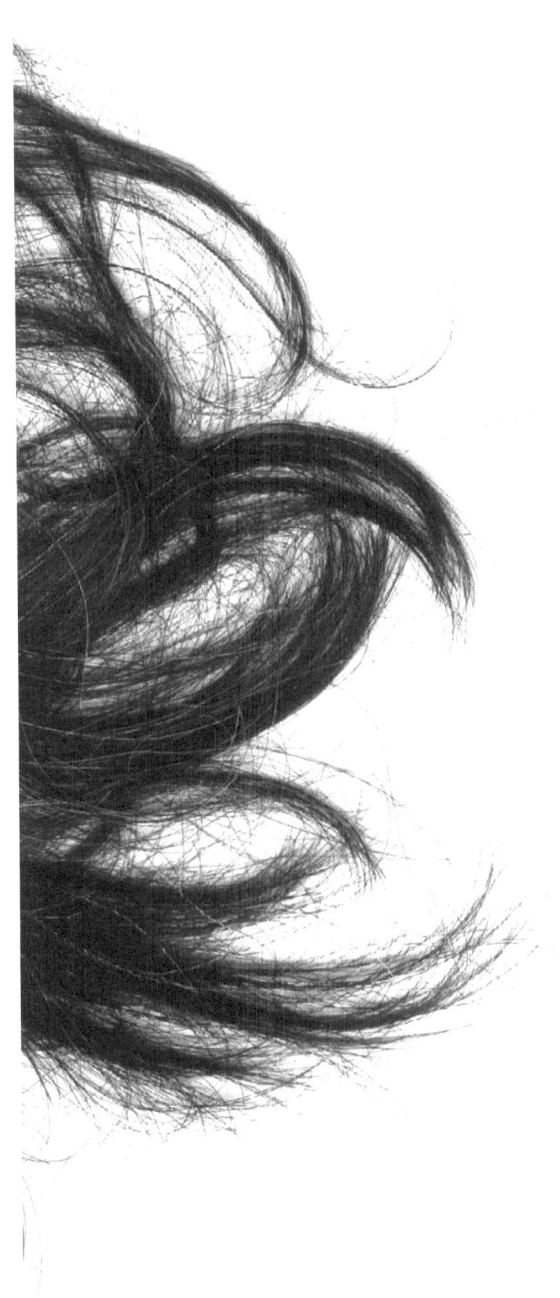

Carola Clift

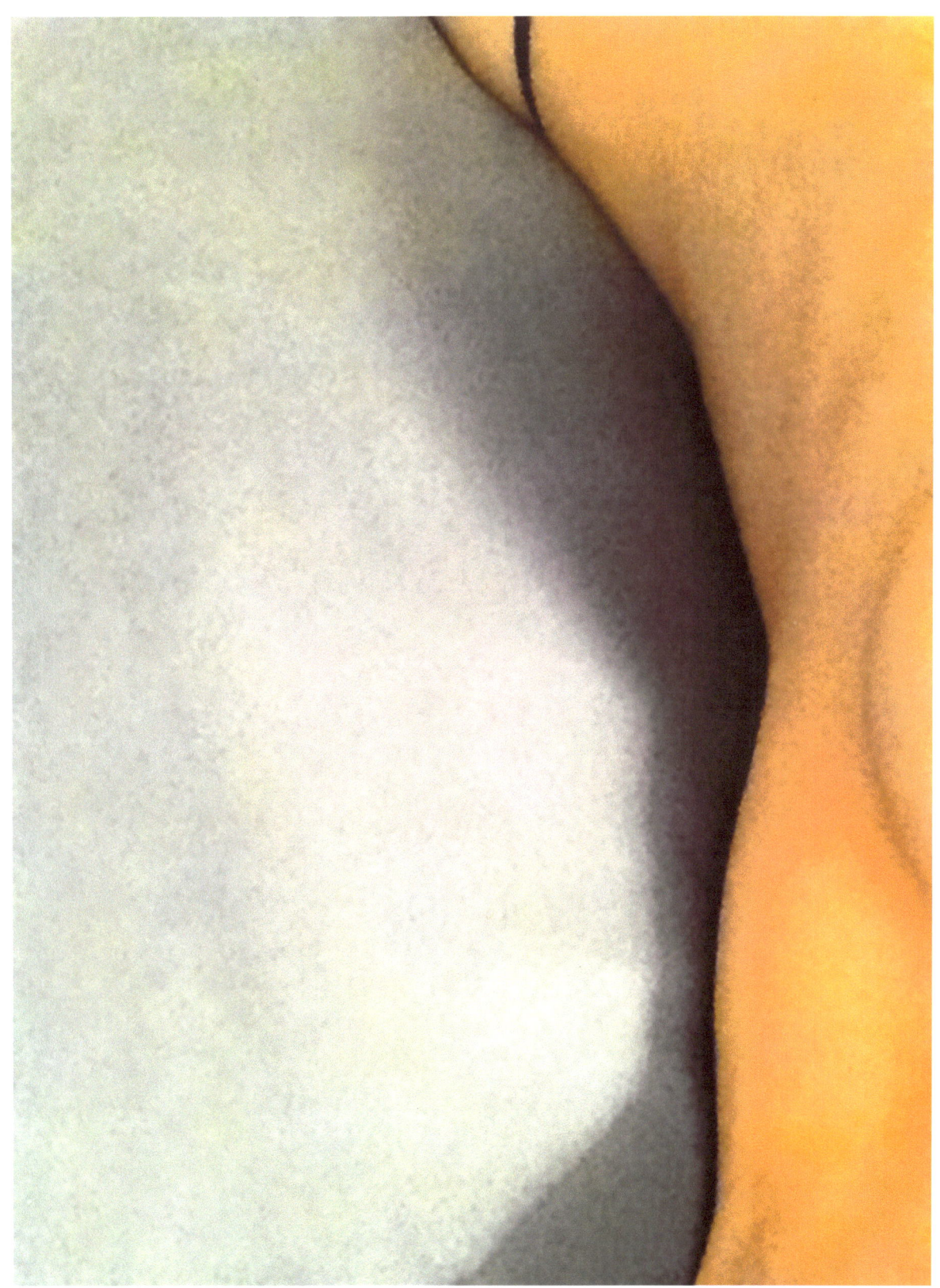

William Clift

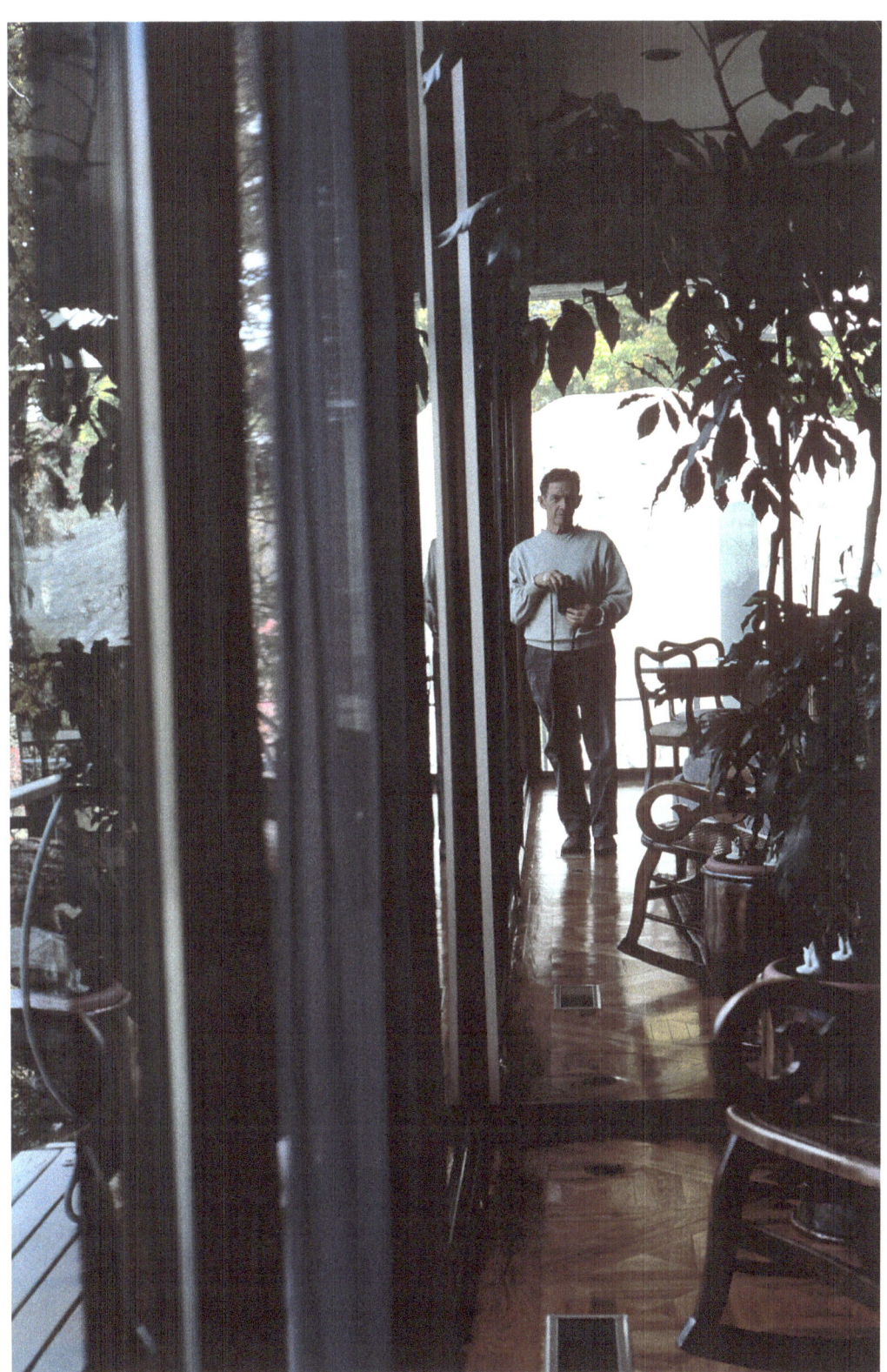

Eric Cousineau

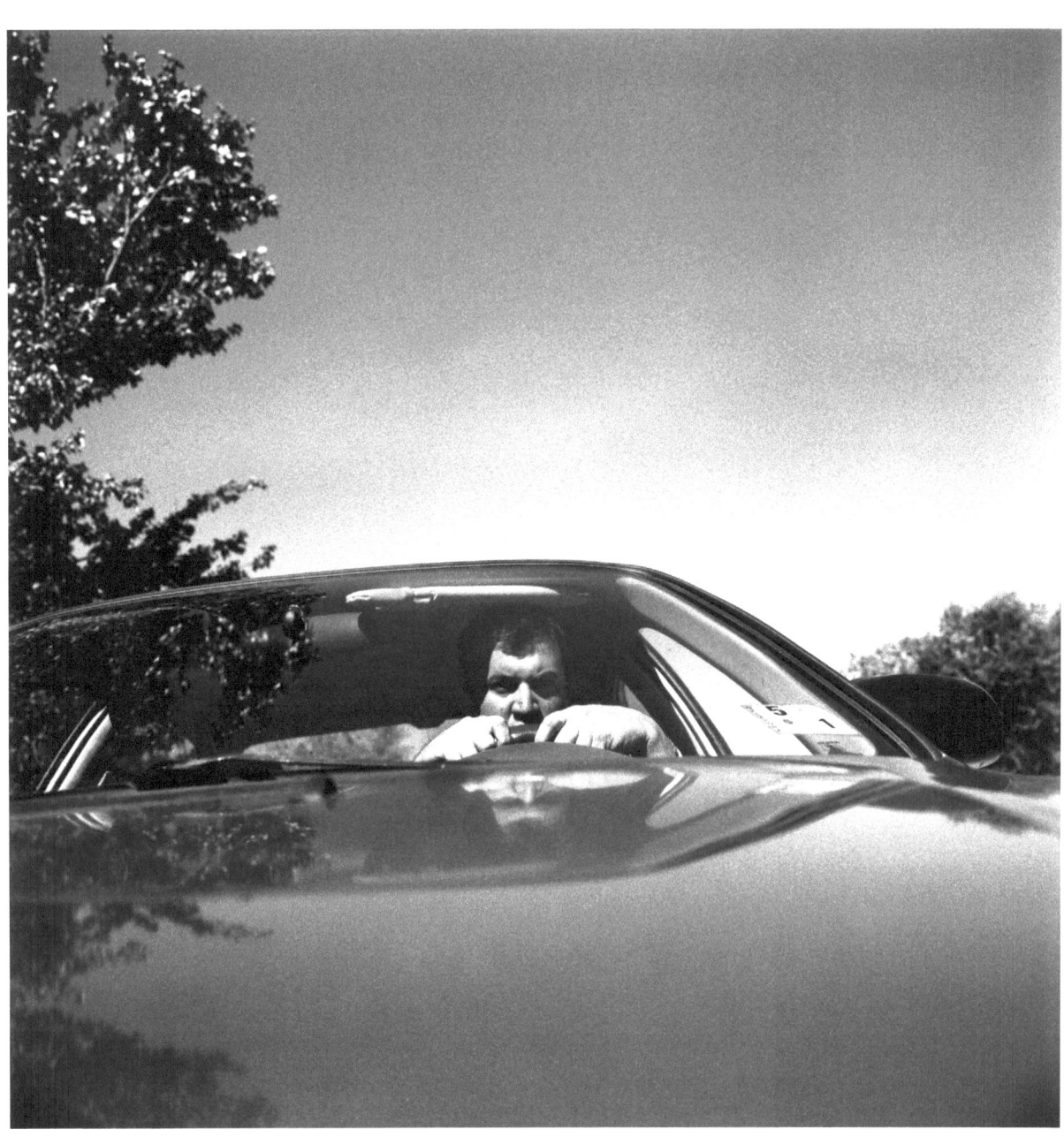

Guy Cross

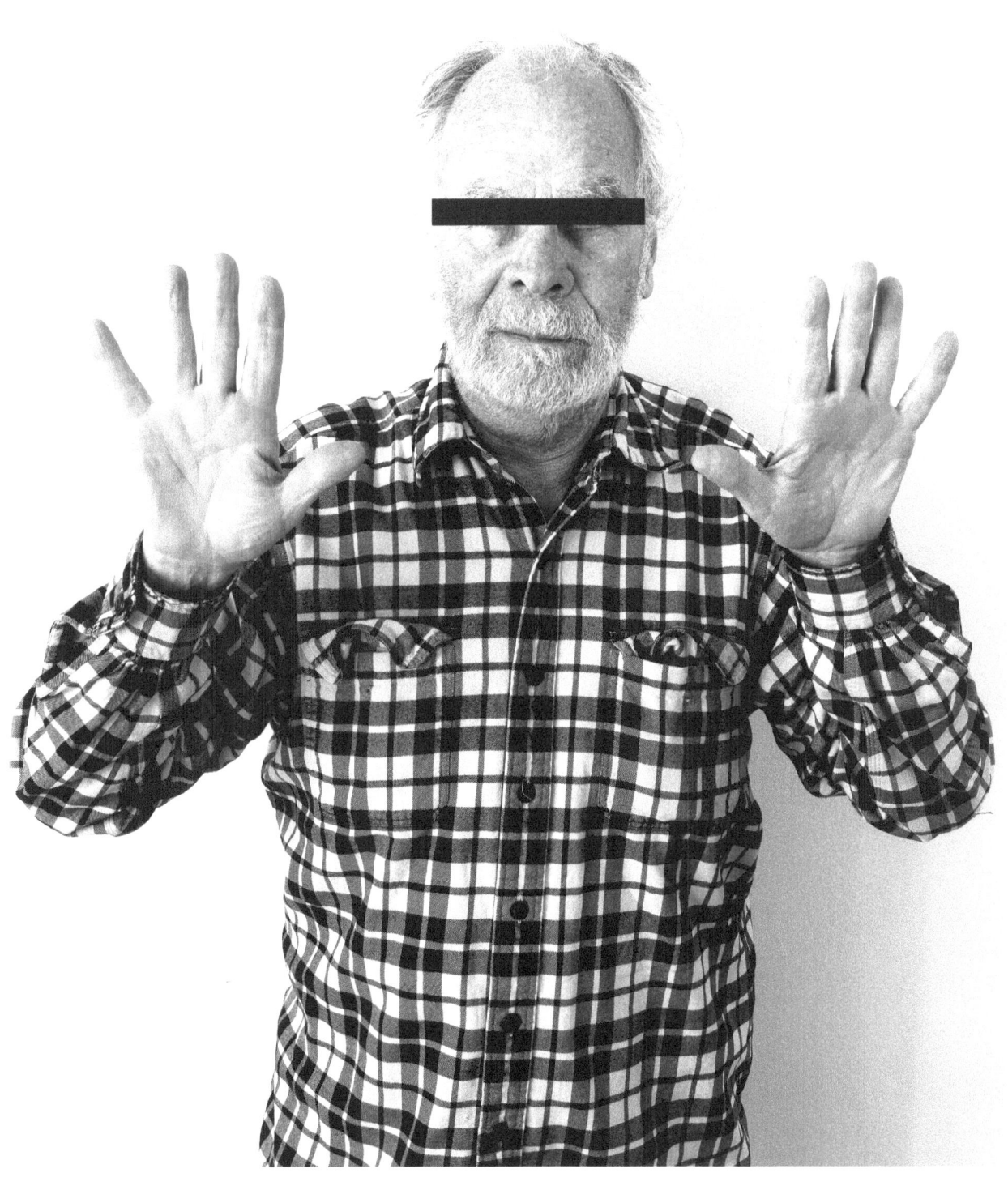

Ungelbah Davila

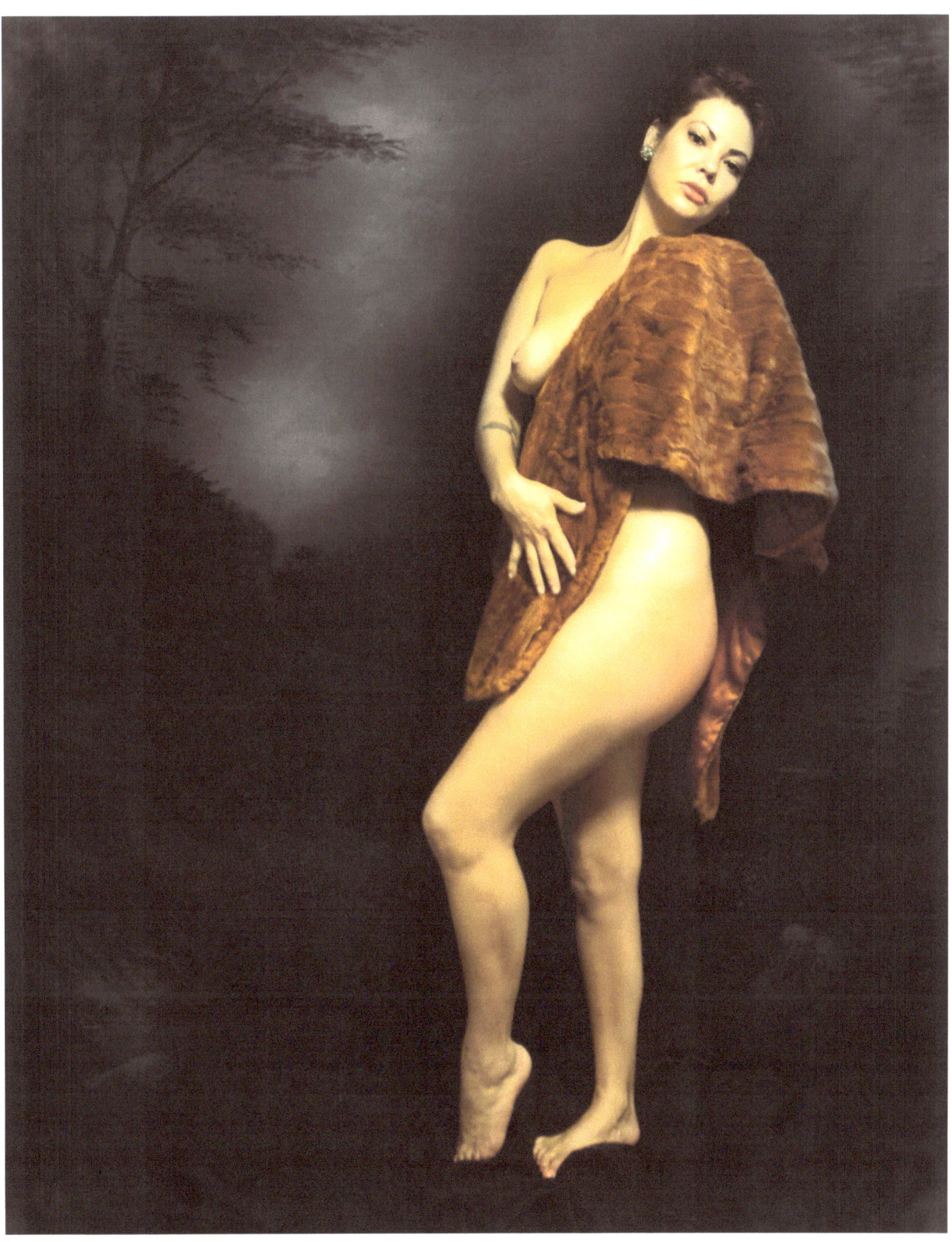

Antone Dolezal

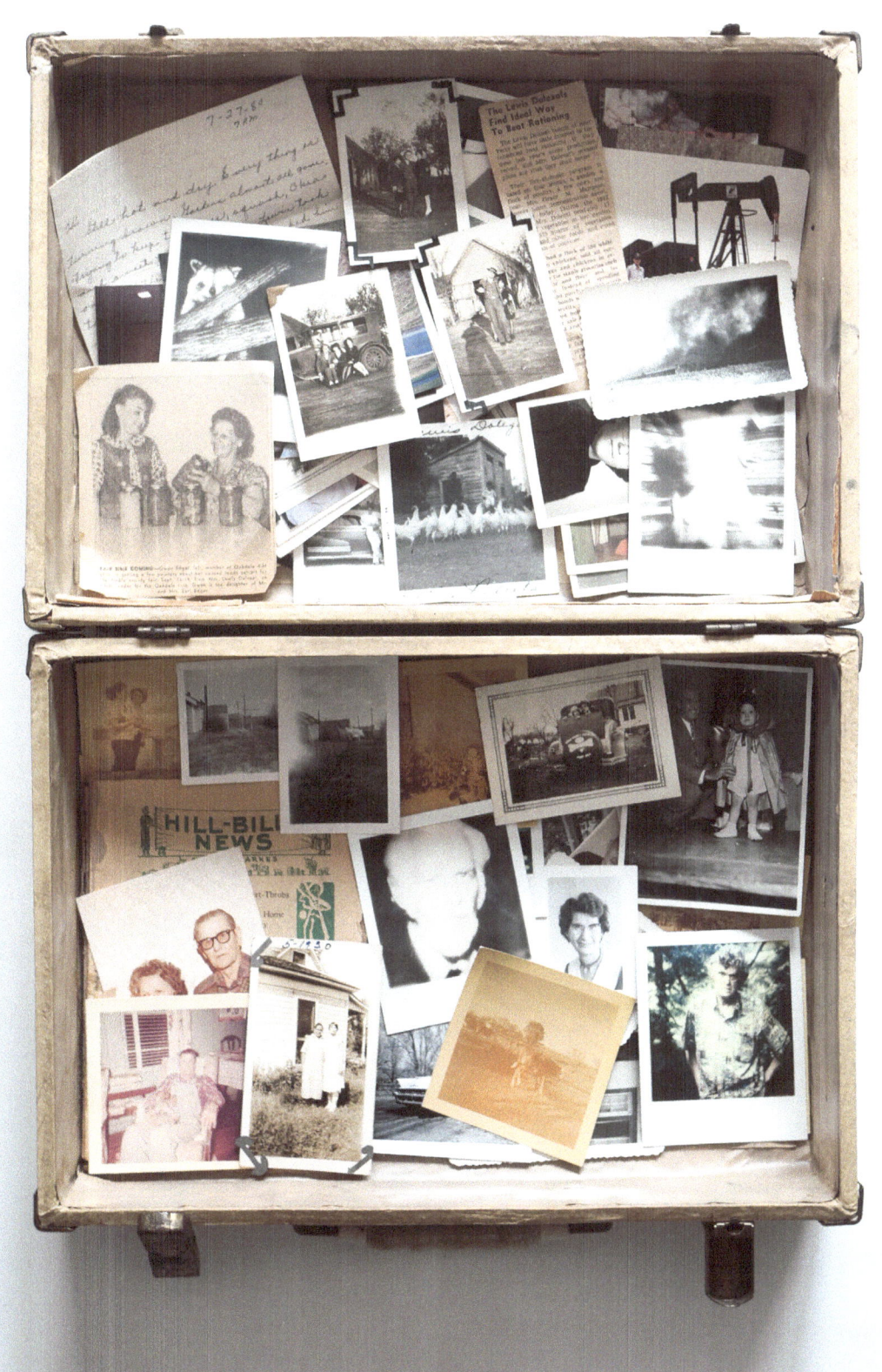

Dianne Duenzl

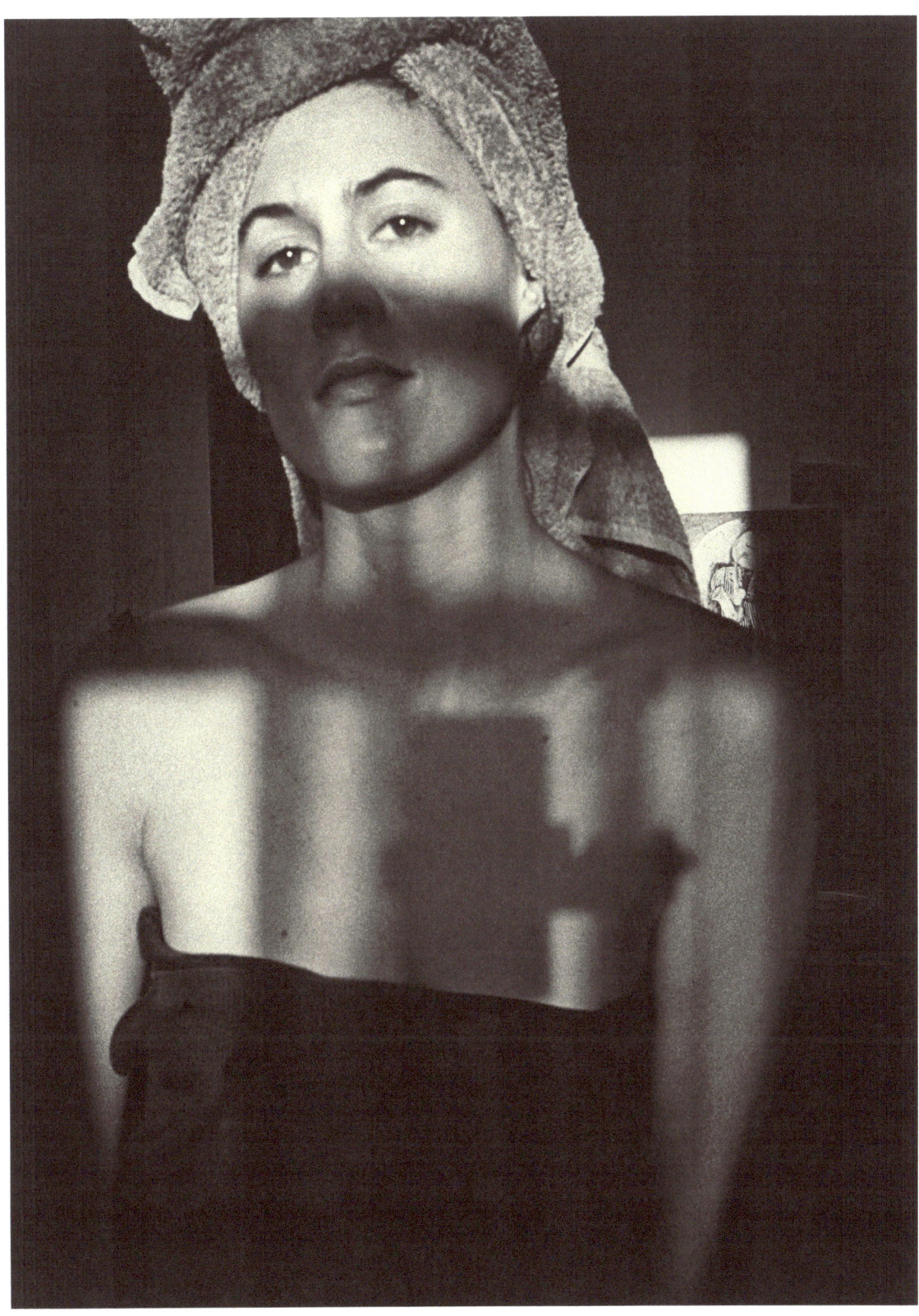

Jennifer Esperanza

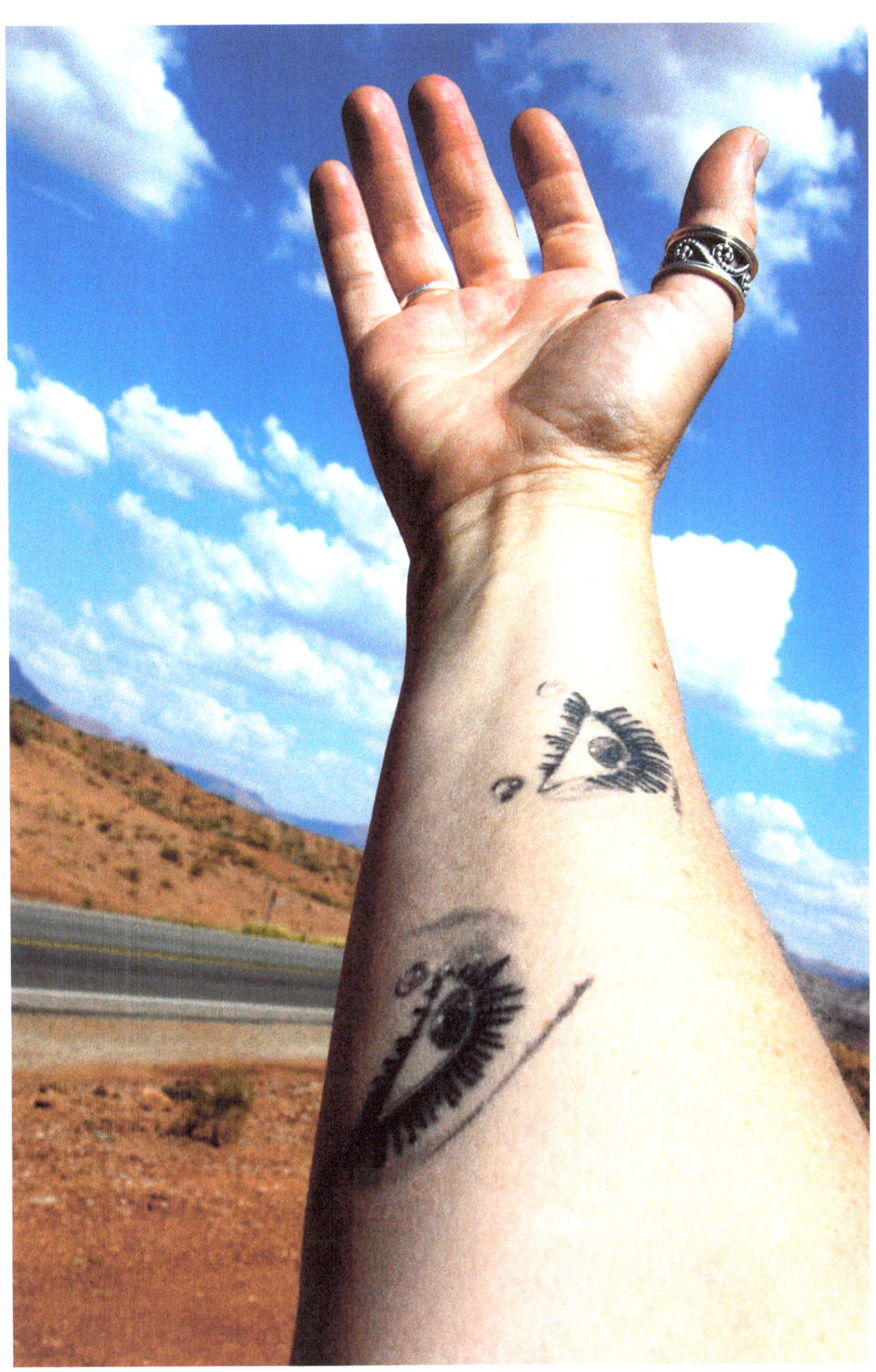

Steve Fitch

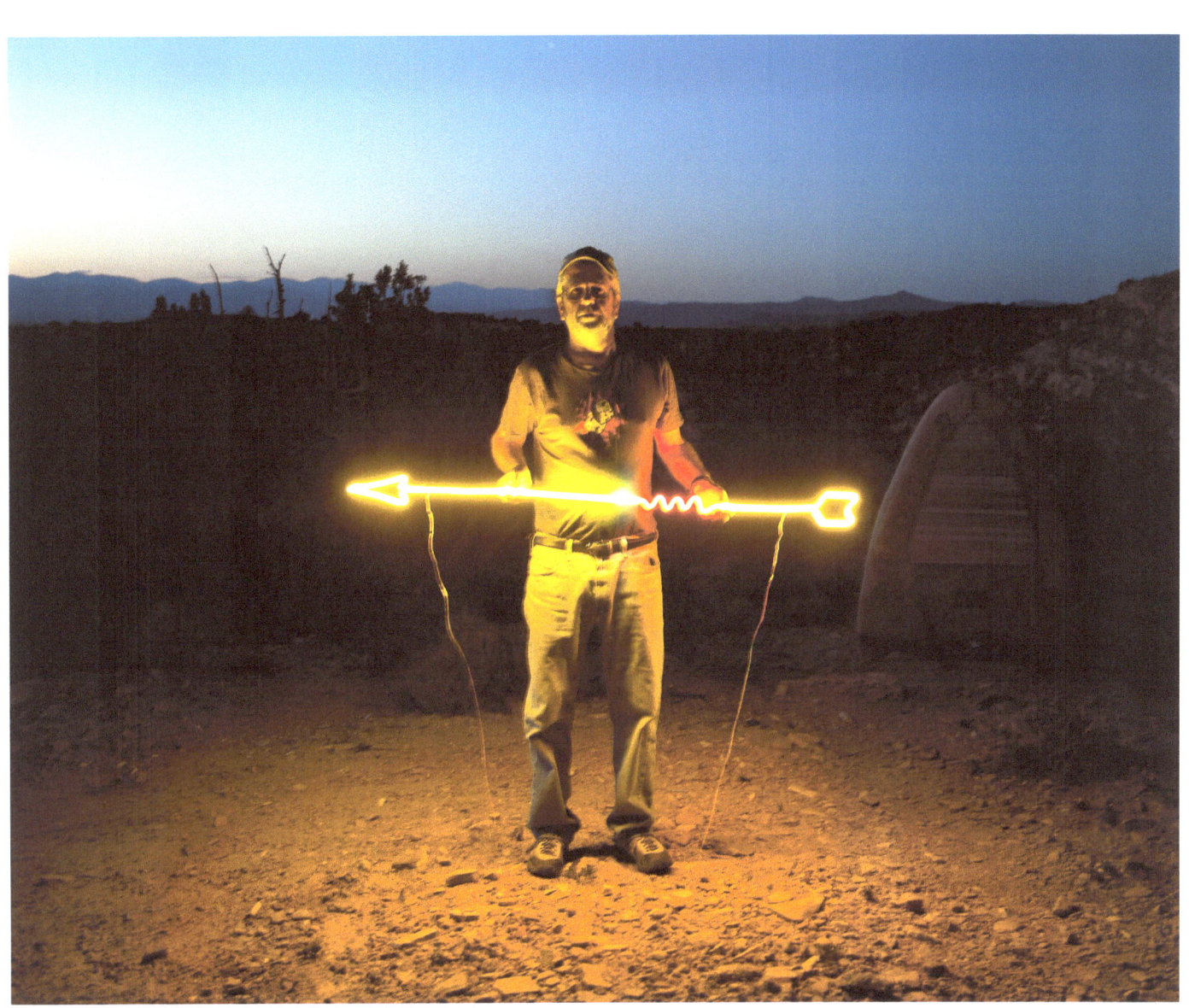

Patricia Galagan

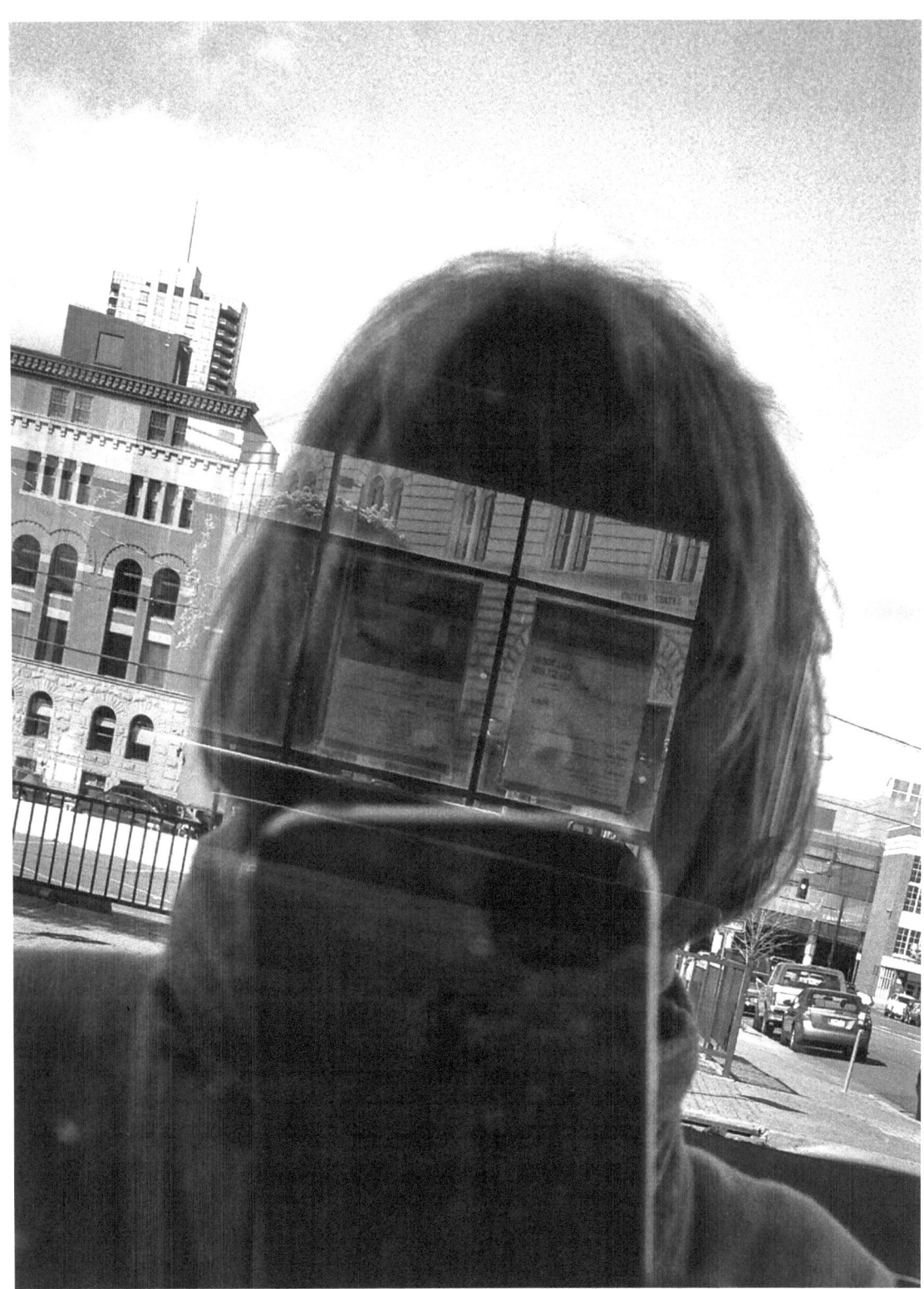

Kirk Gittings

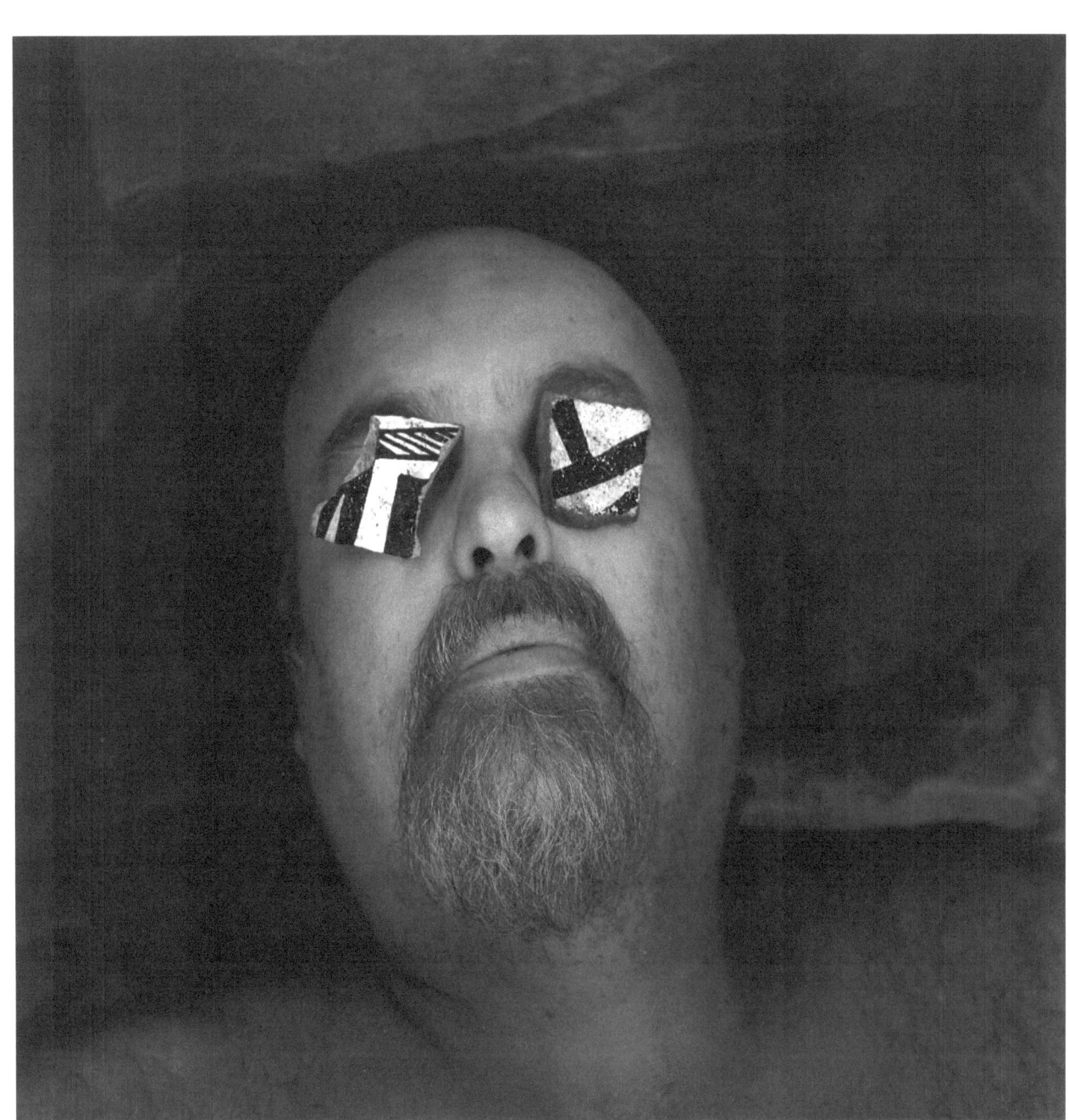

Lydia Gonzales

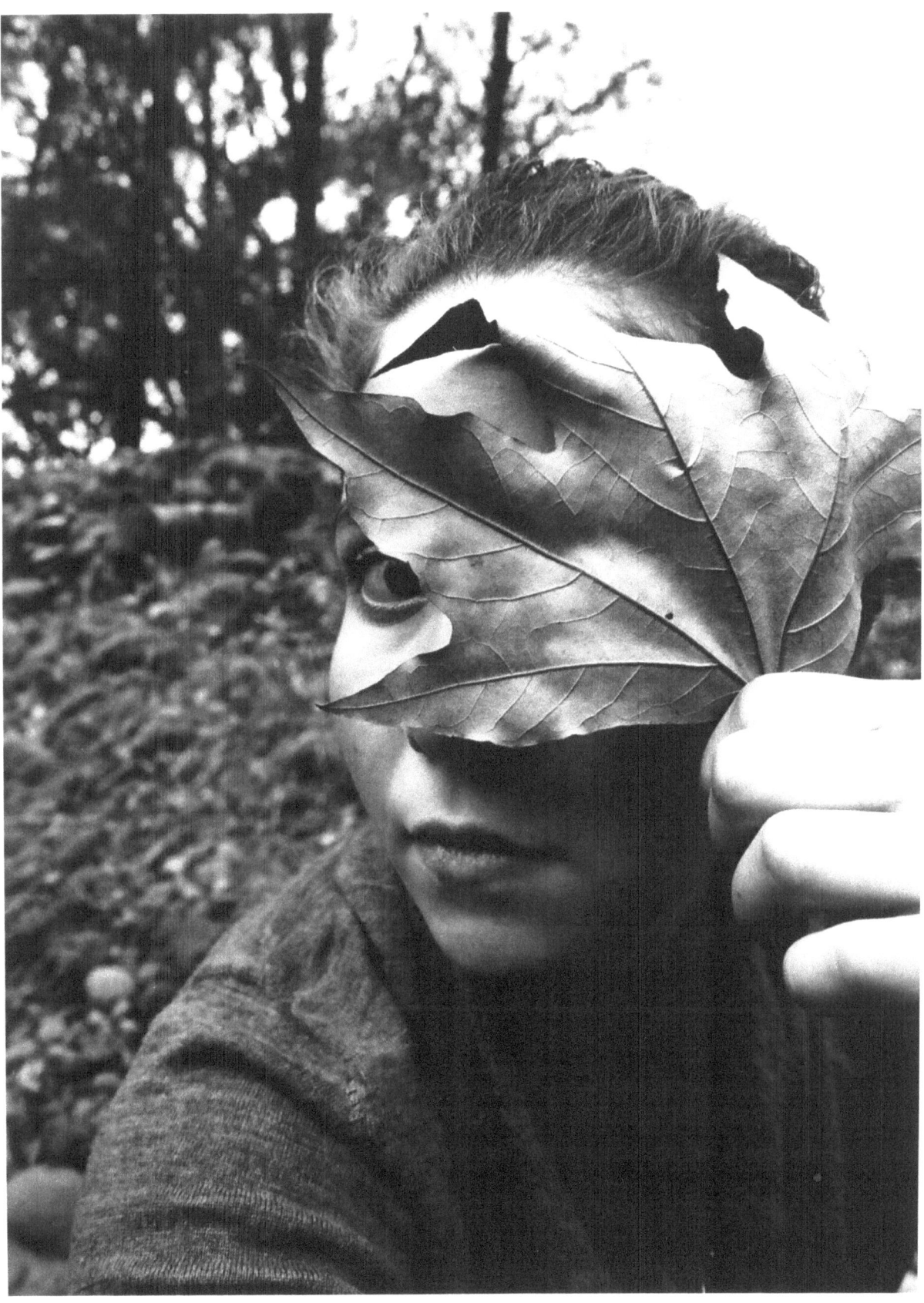

Sondra Goodwin

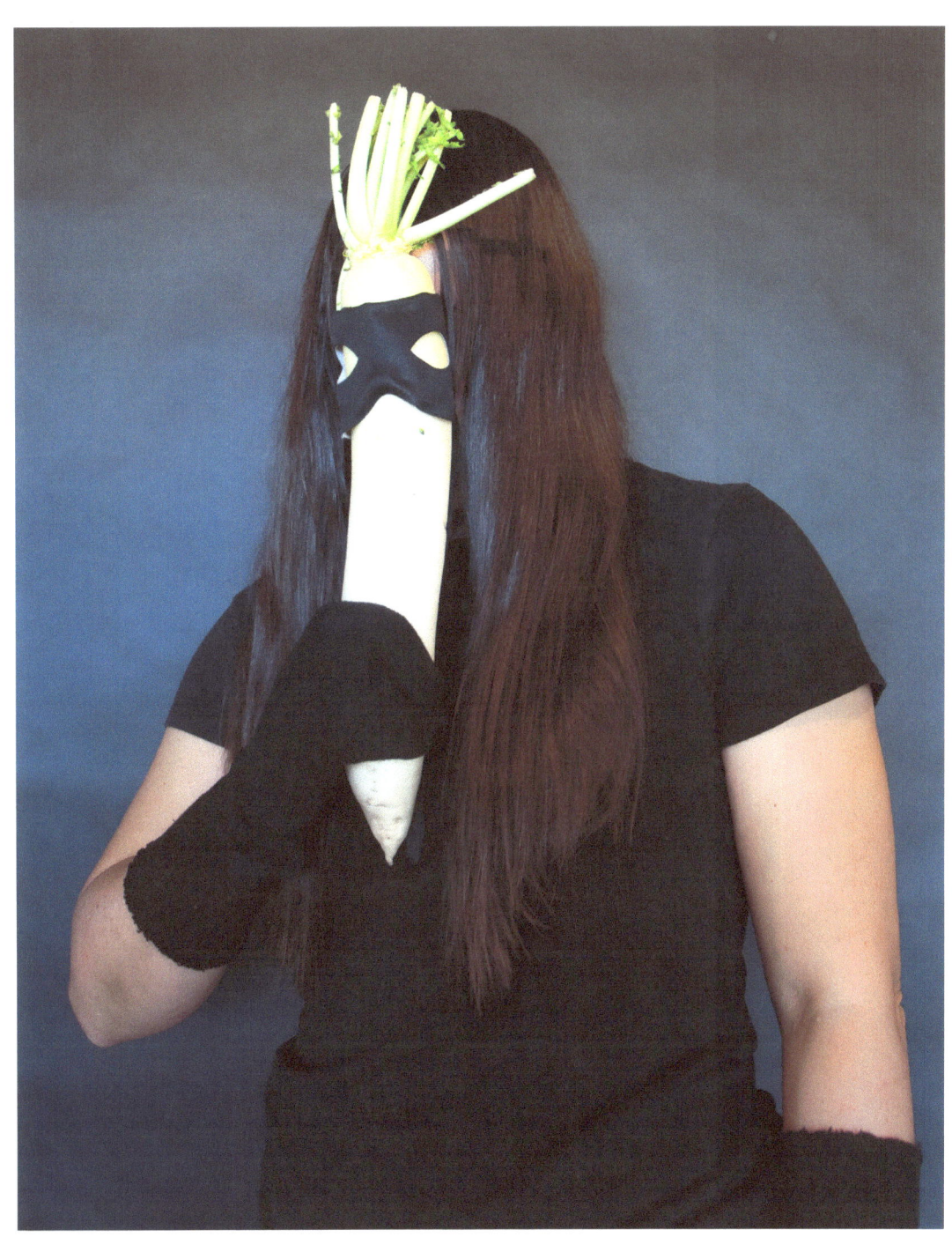

Meggan Gould

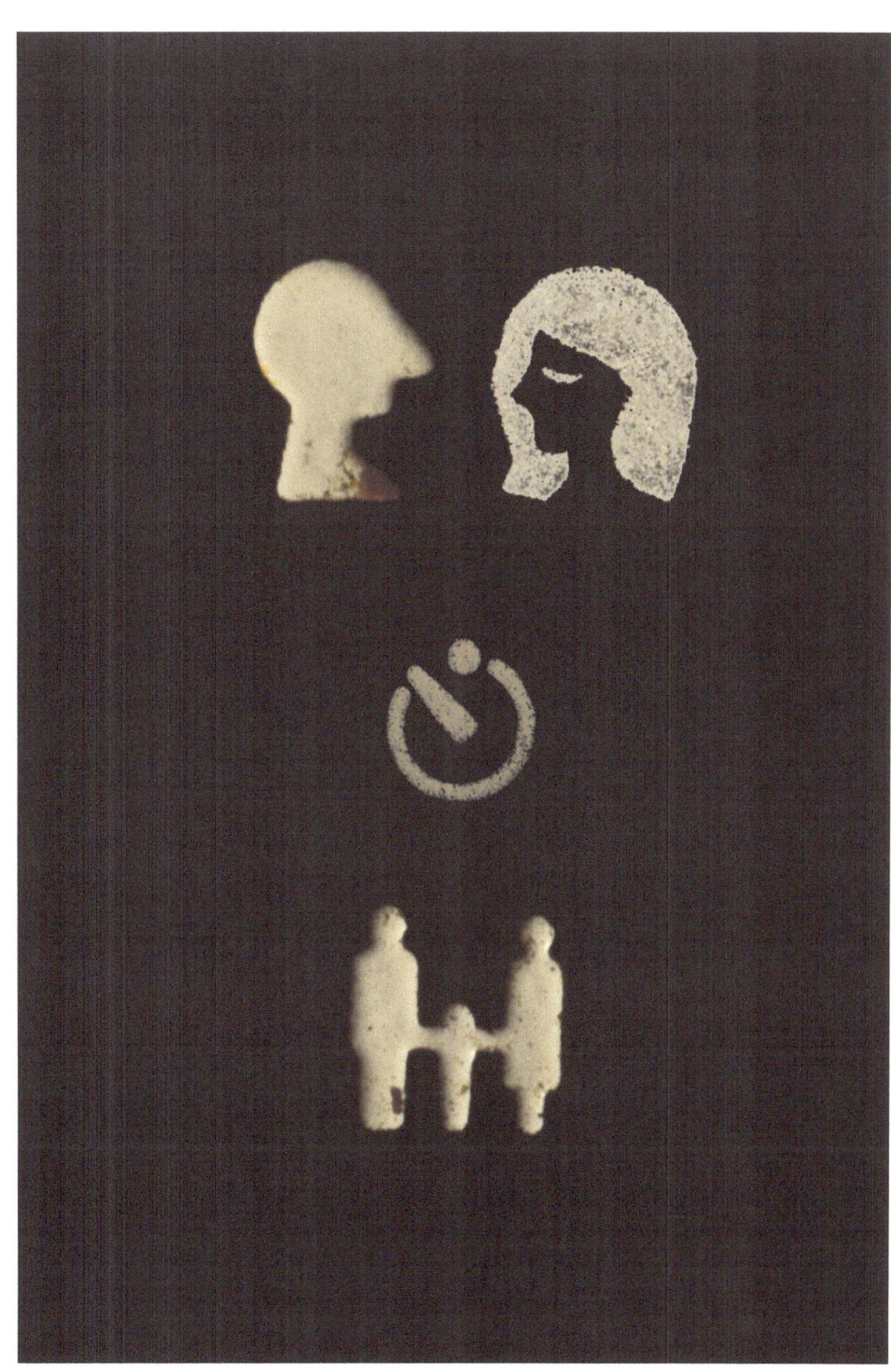

Lauren Greenwald

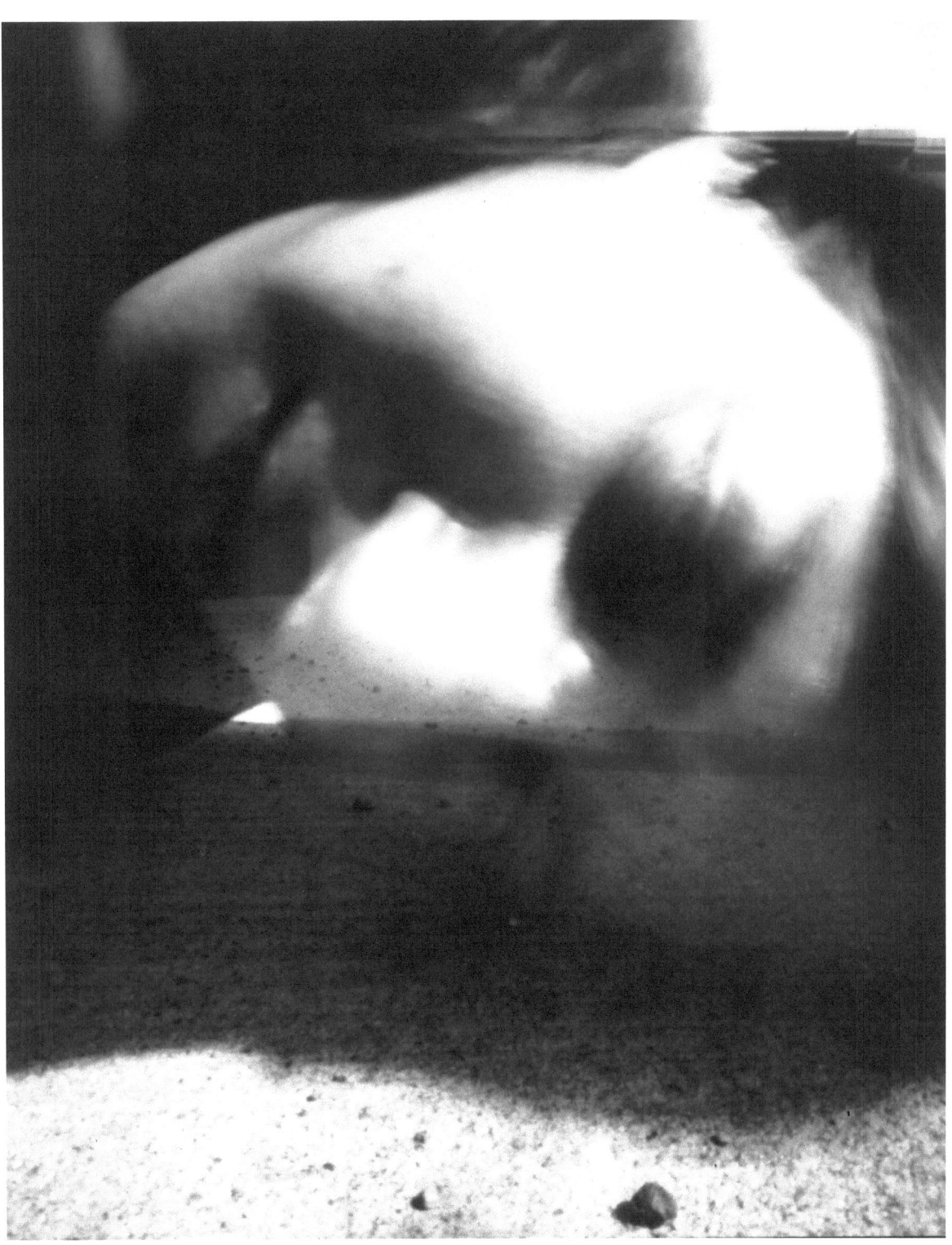

James Hart

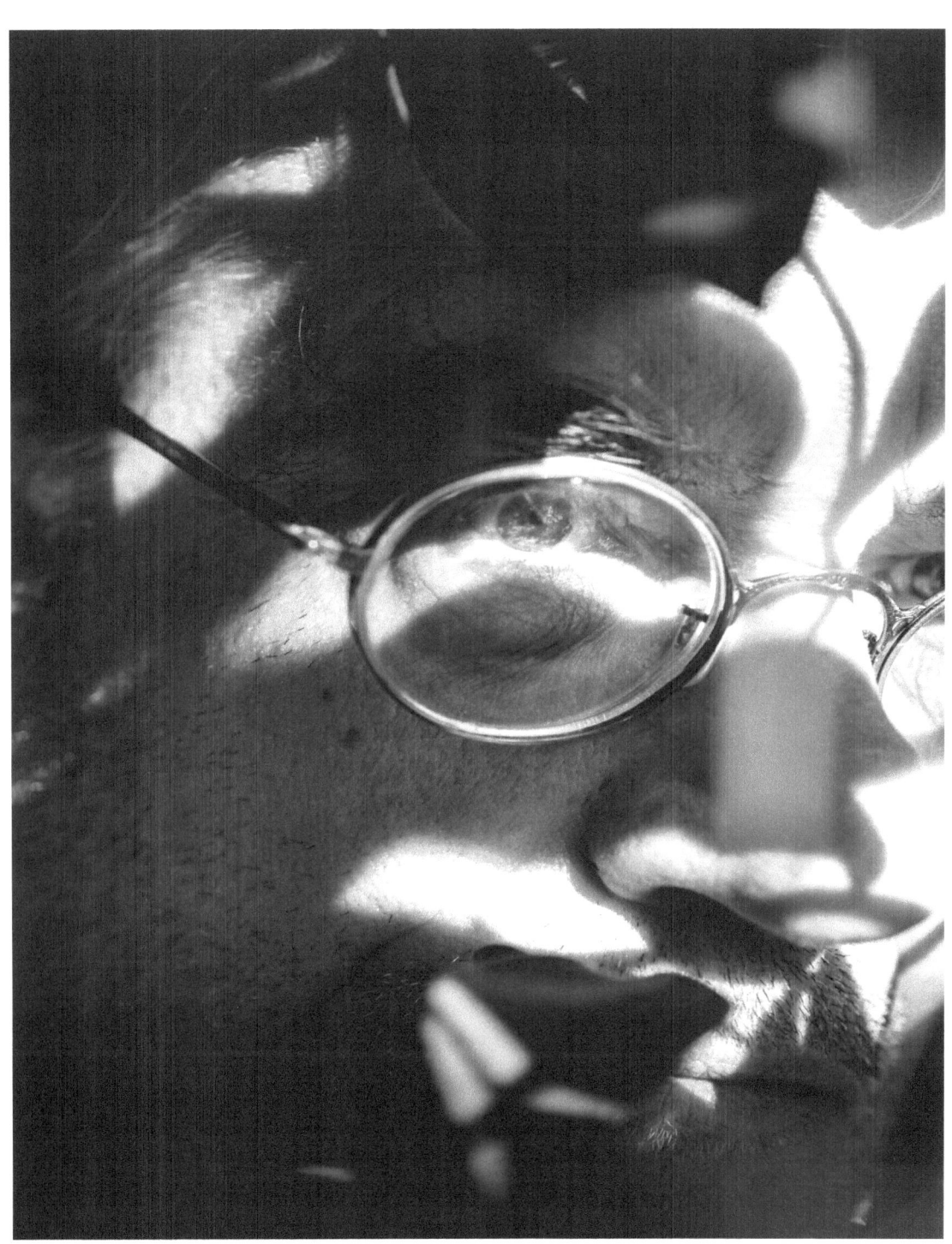

Sol Hill

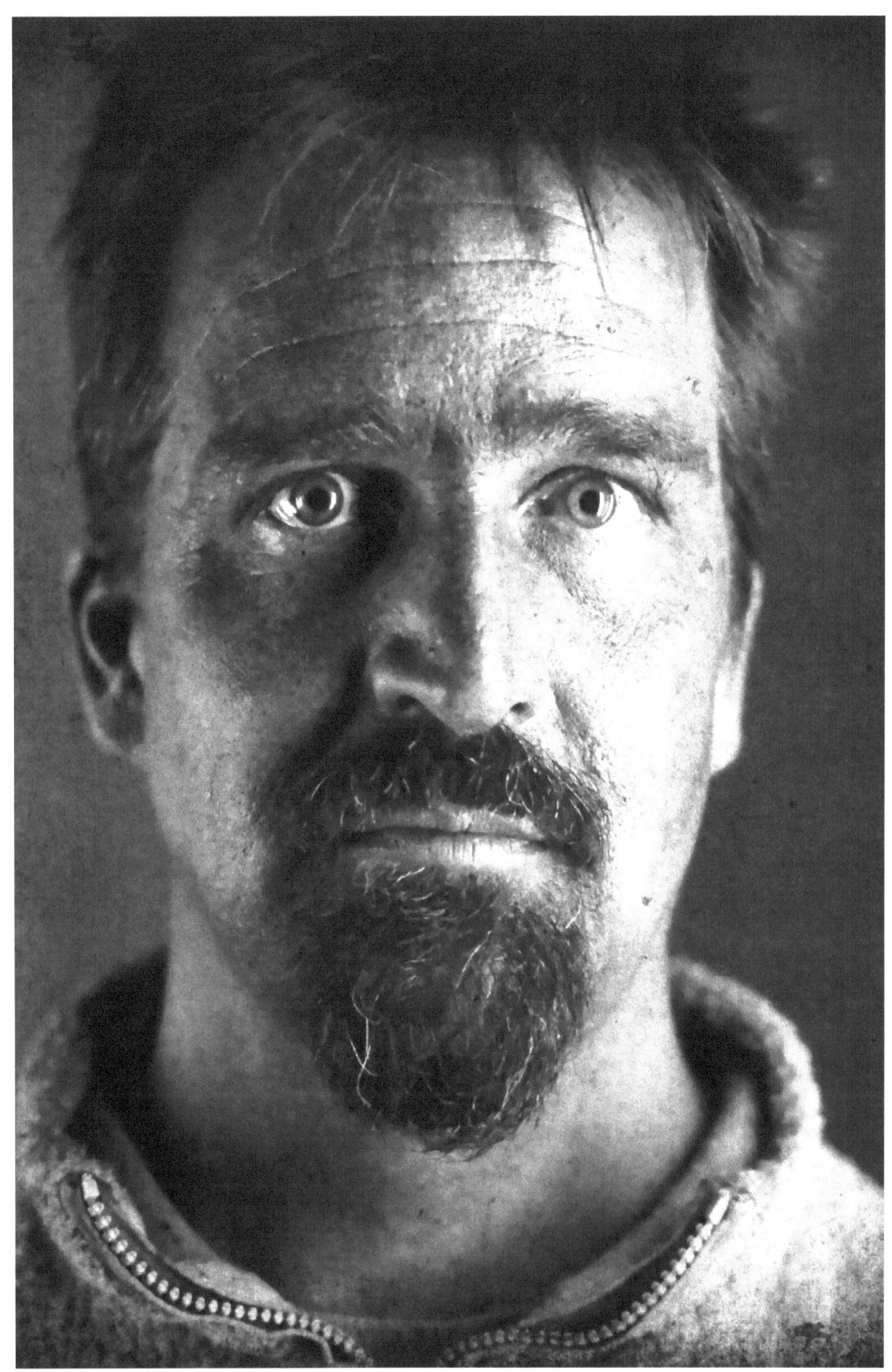

Megan Jacobs

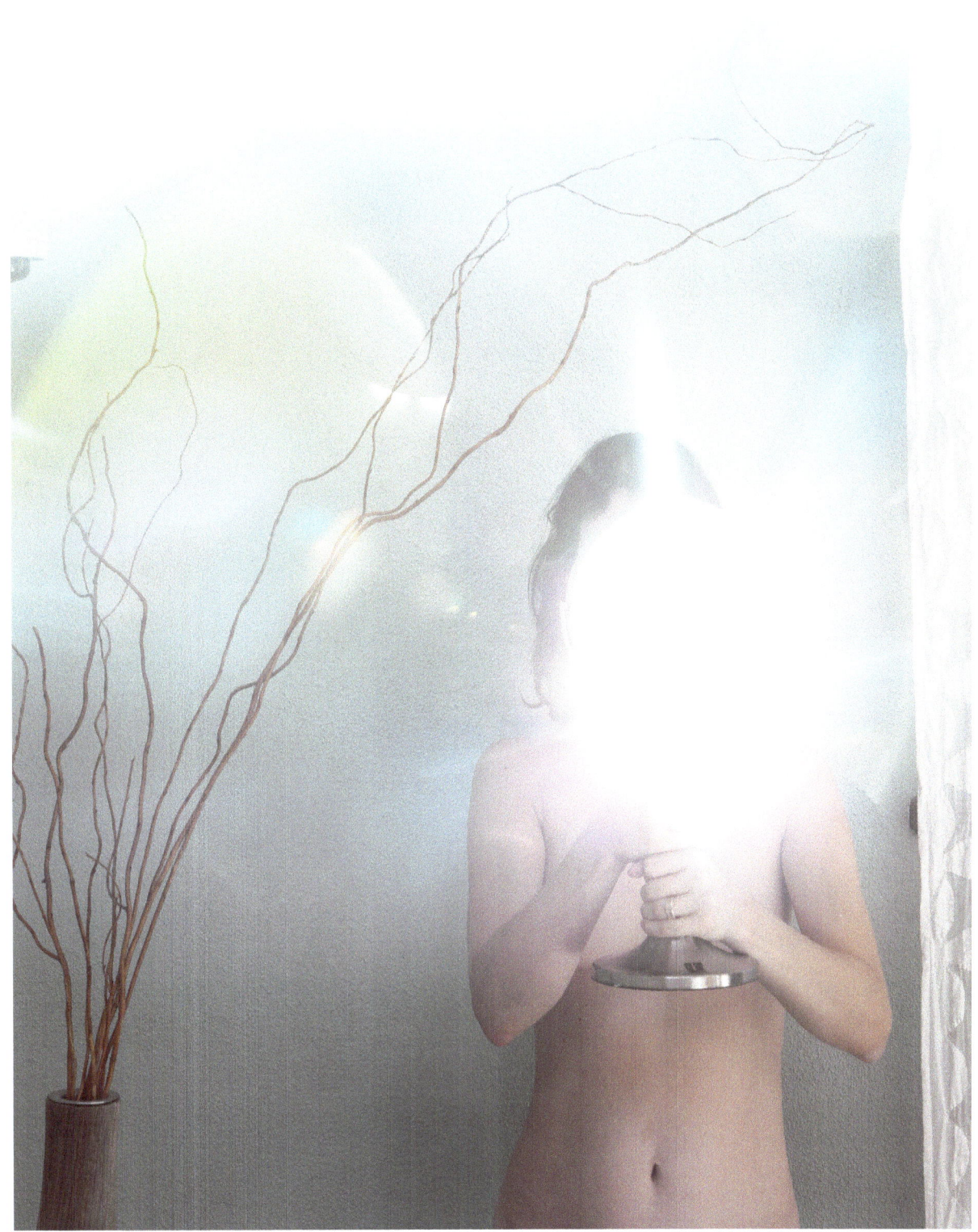

Jen Judge

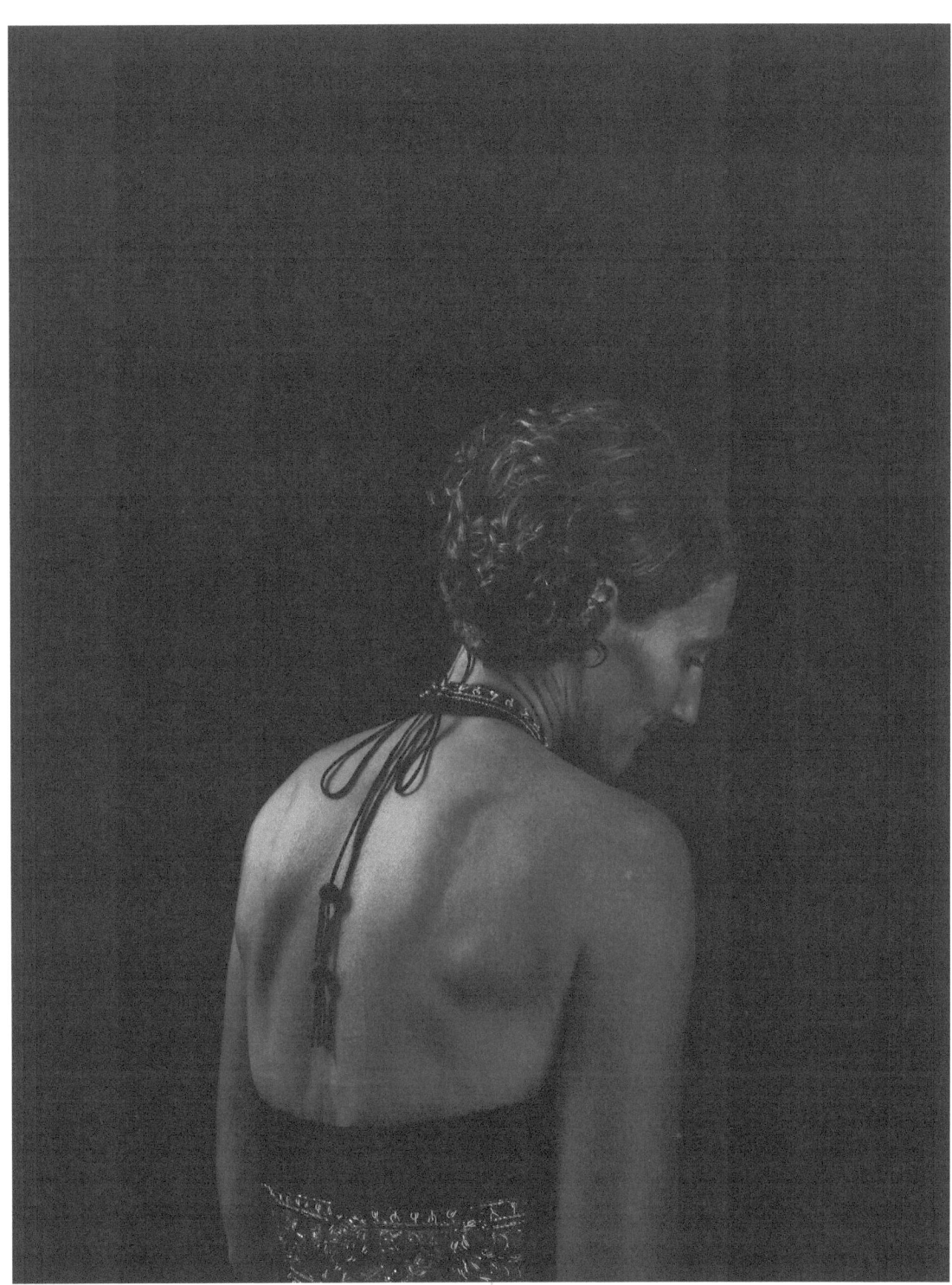

David Michael Kennedy

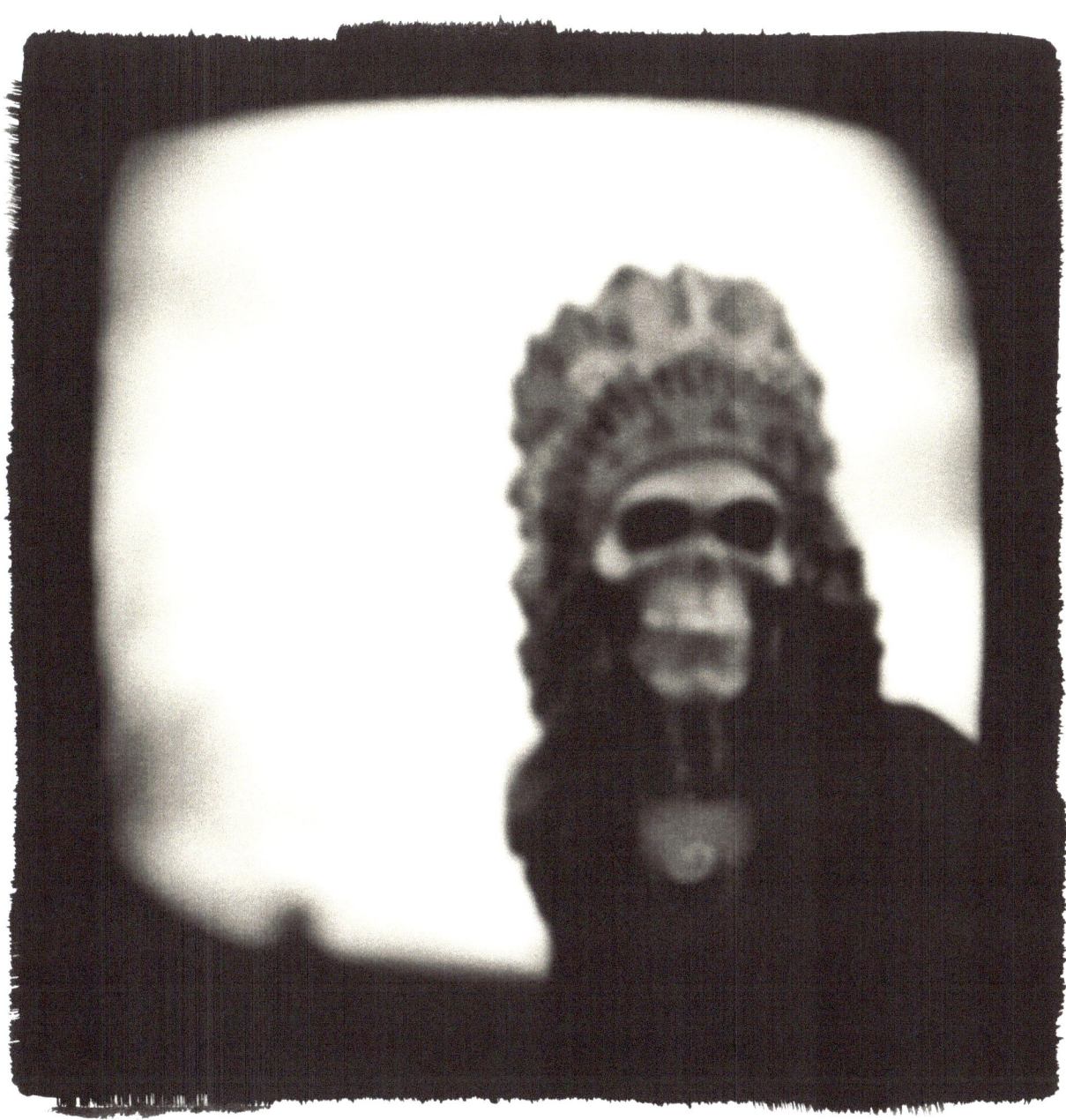

Lisa Law

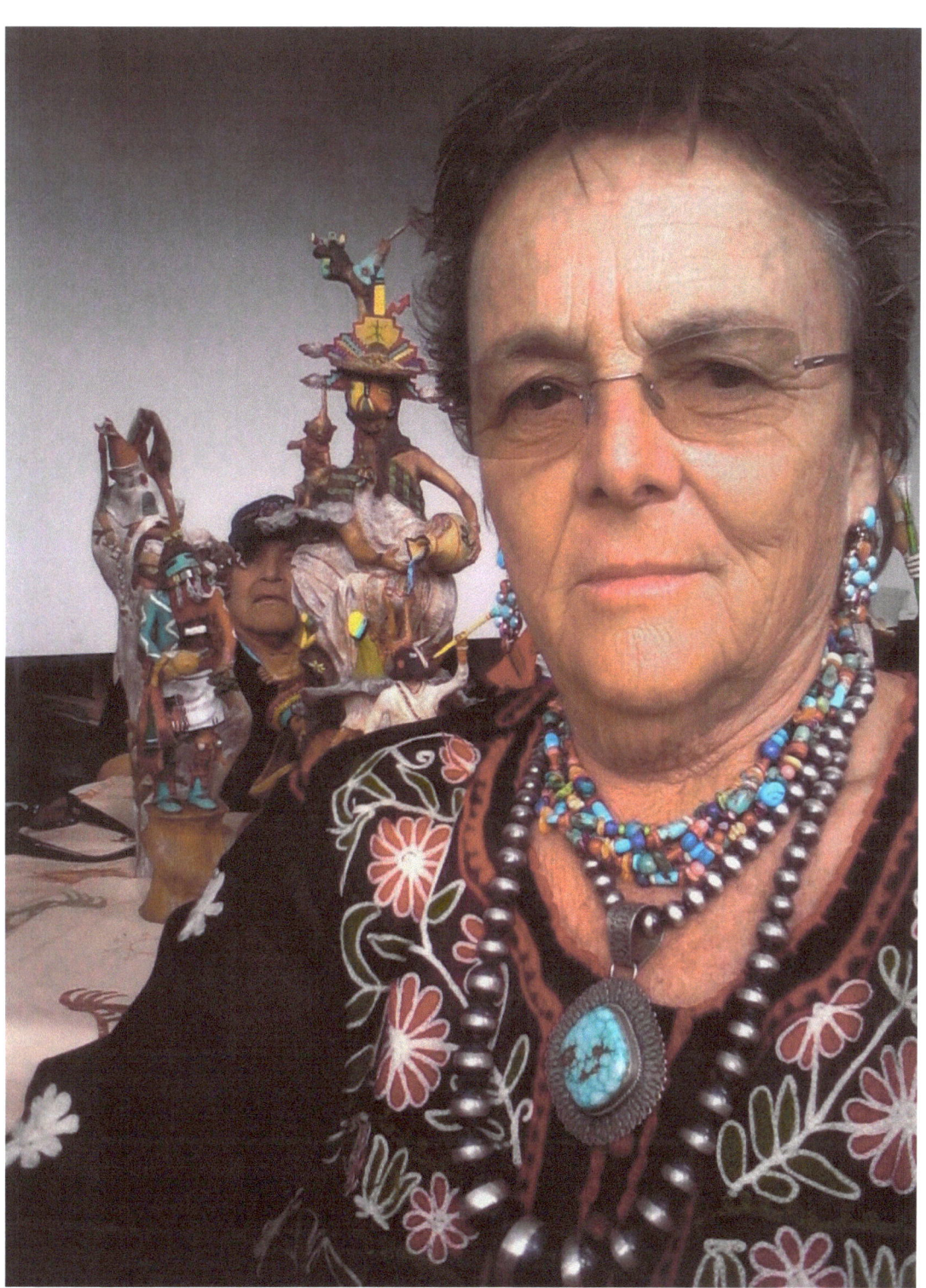

Willis F. Lee

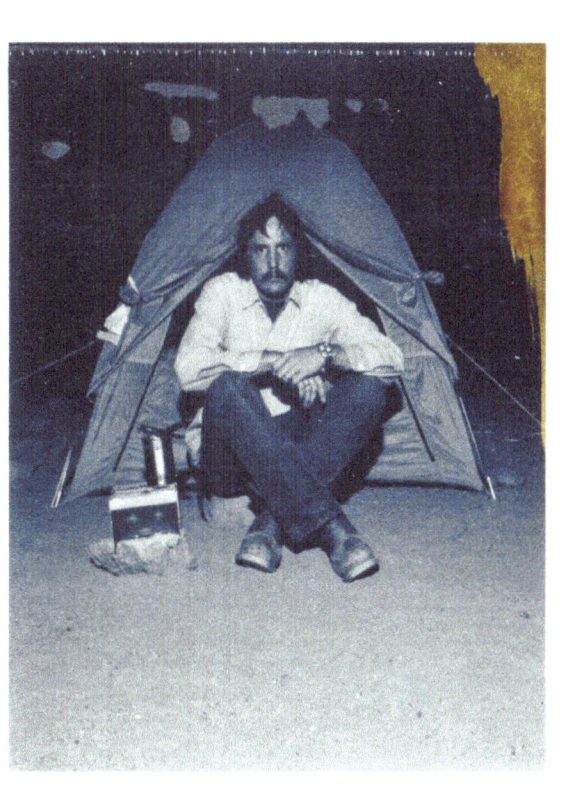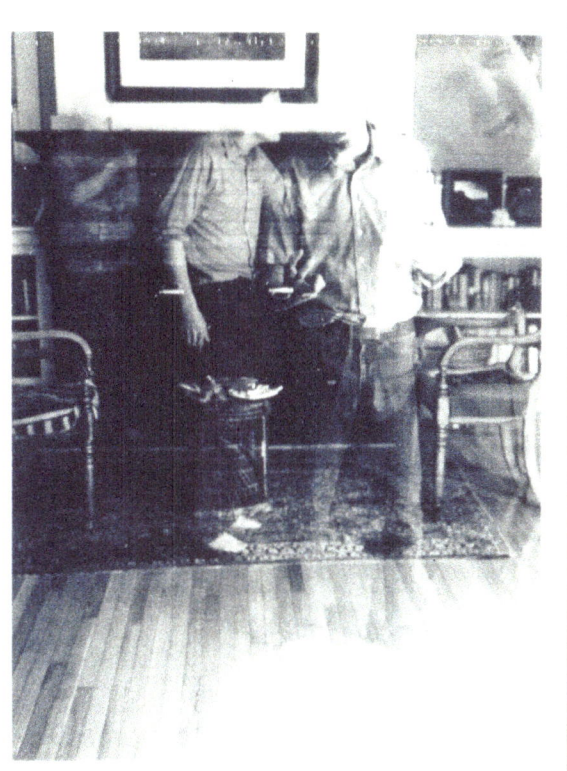

Louis Leray

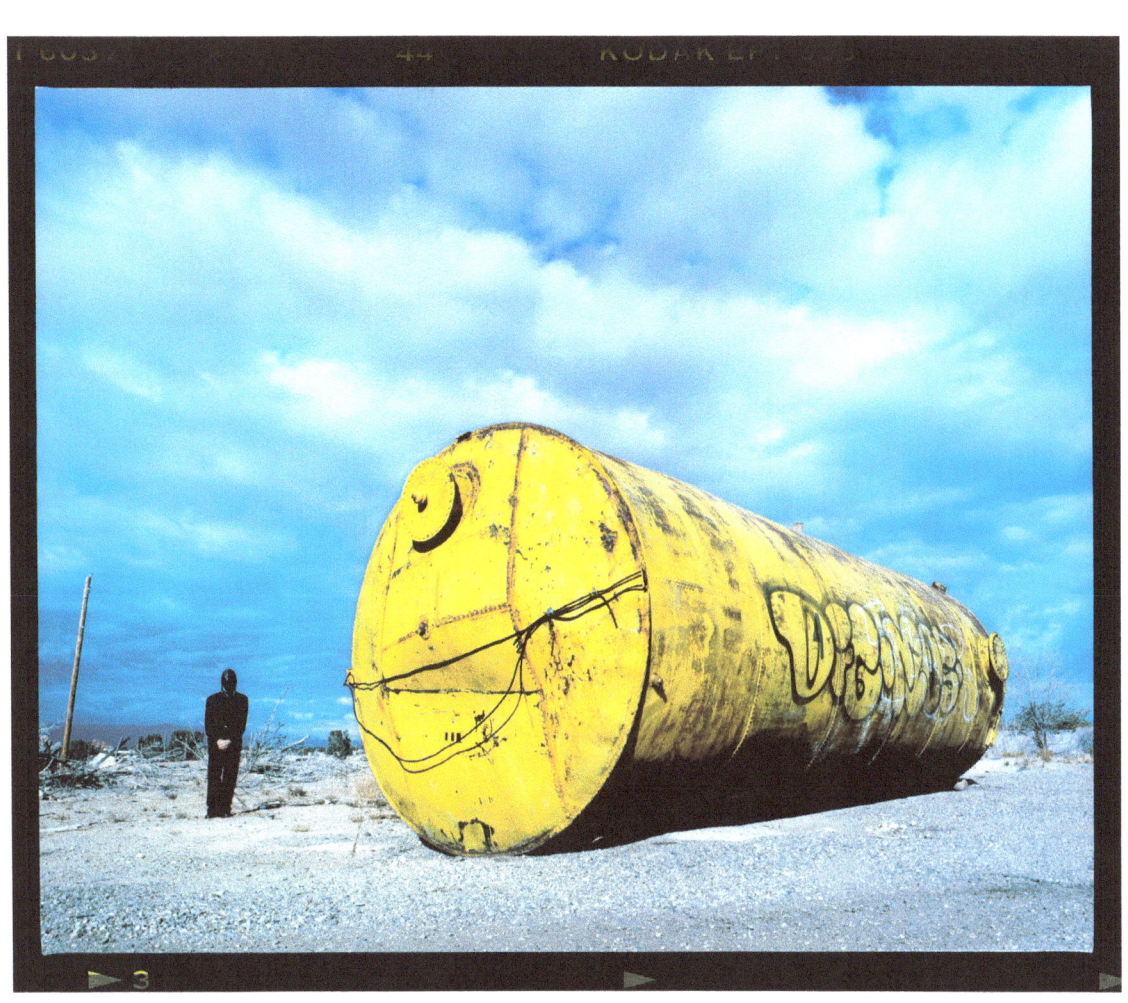

Patti Levey

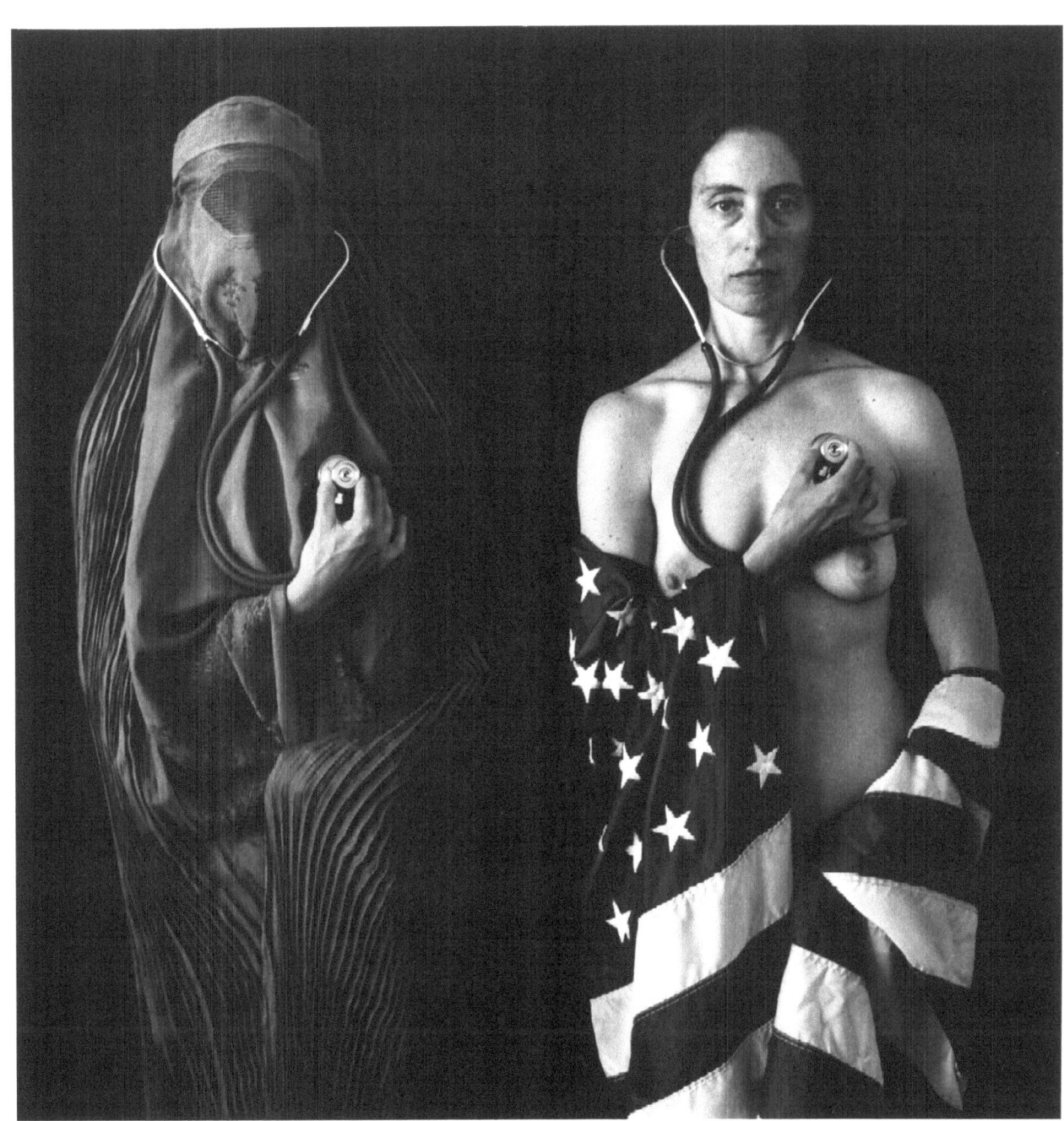

Tamara Lichtenstein

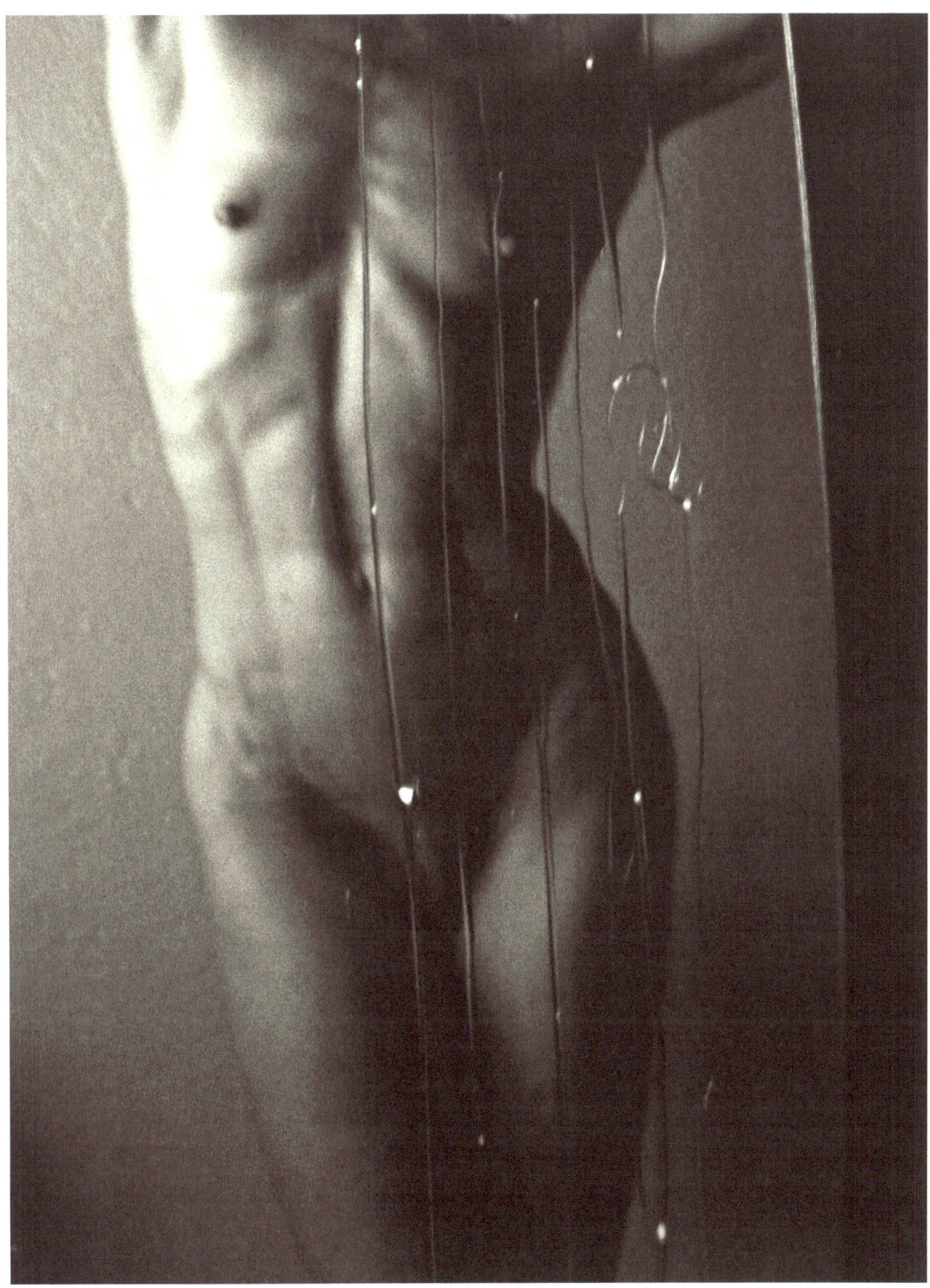

Herbert Lotz

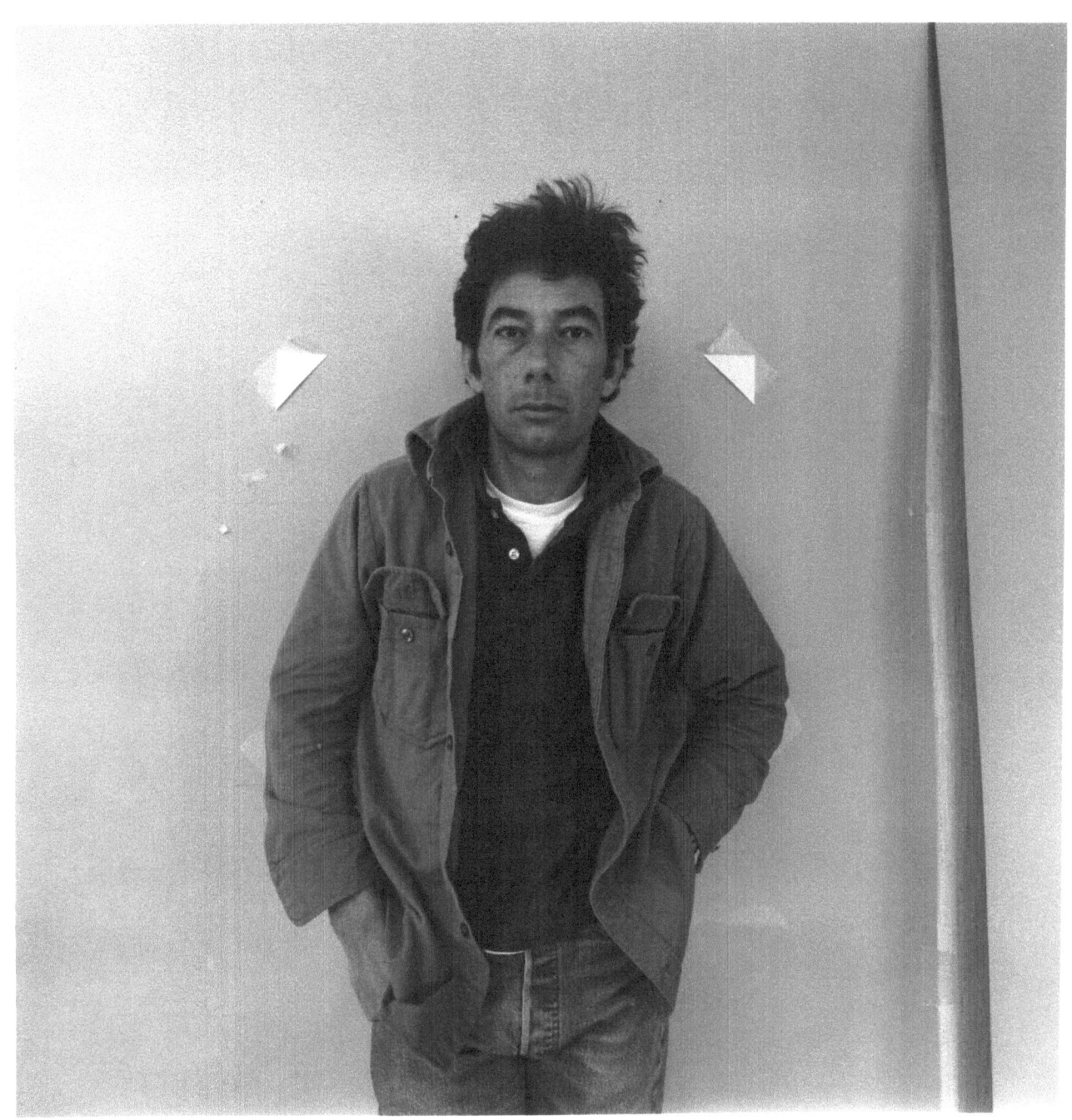

1 9 8 · lot

Jessamyn Lovell

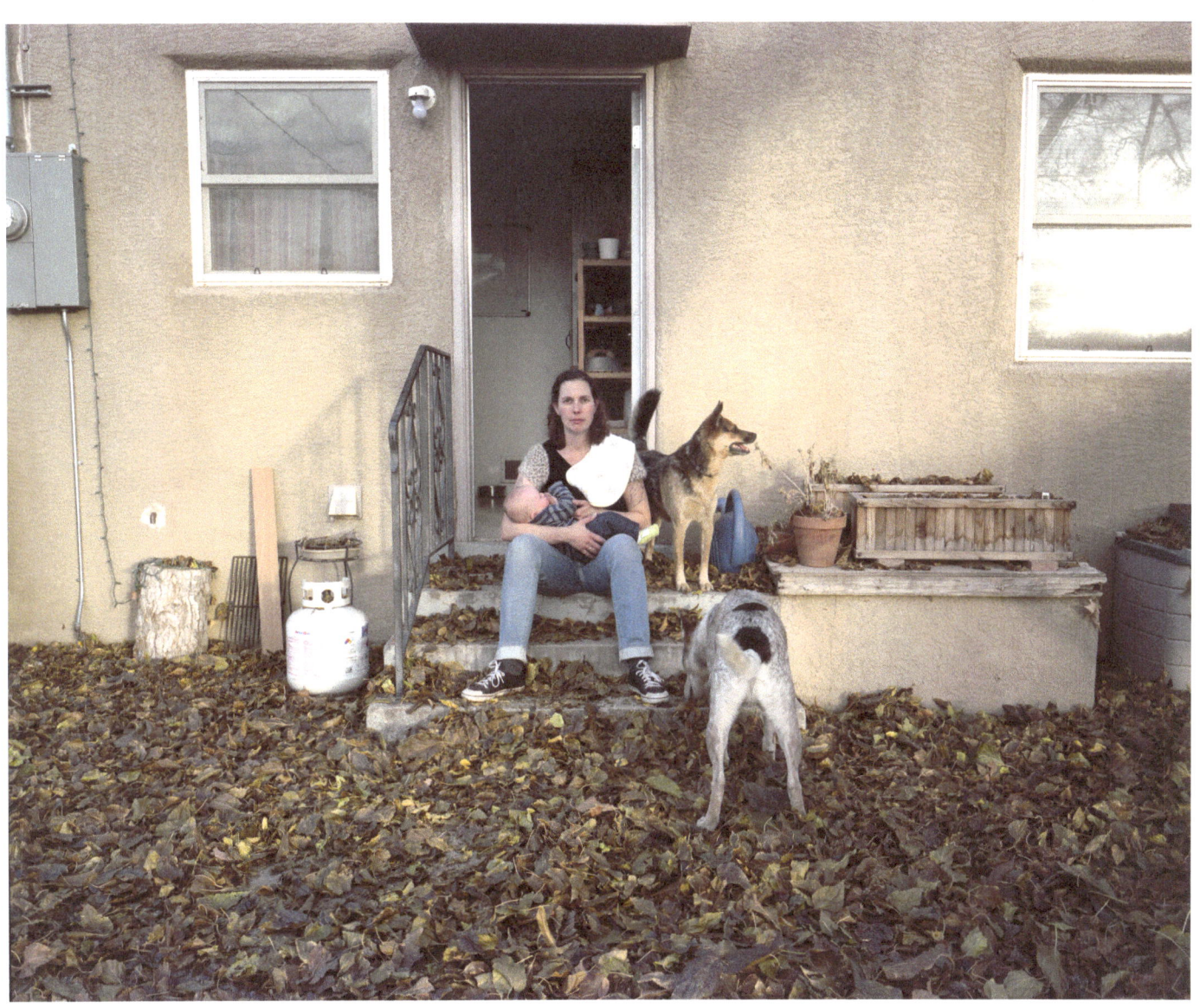

Richard Lowenberg

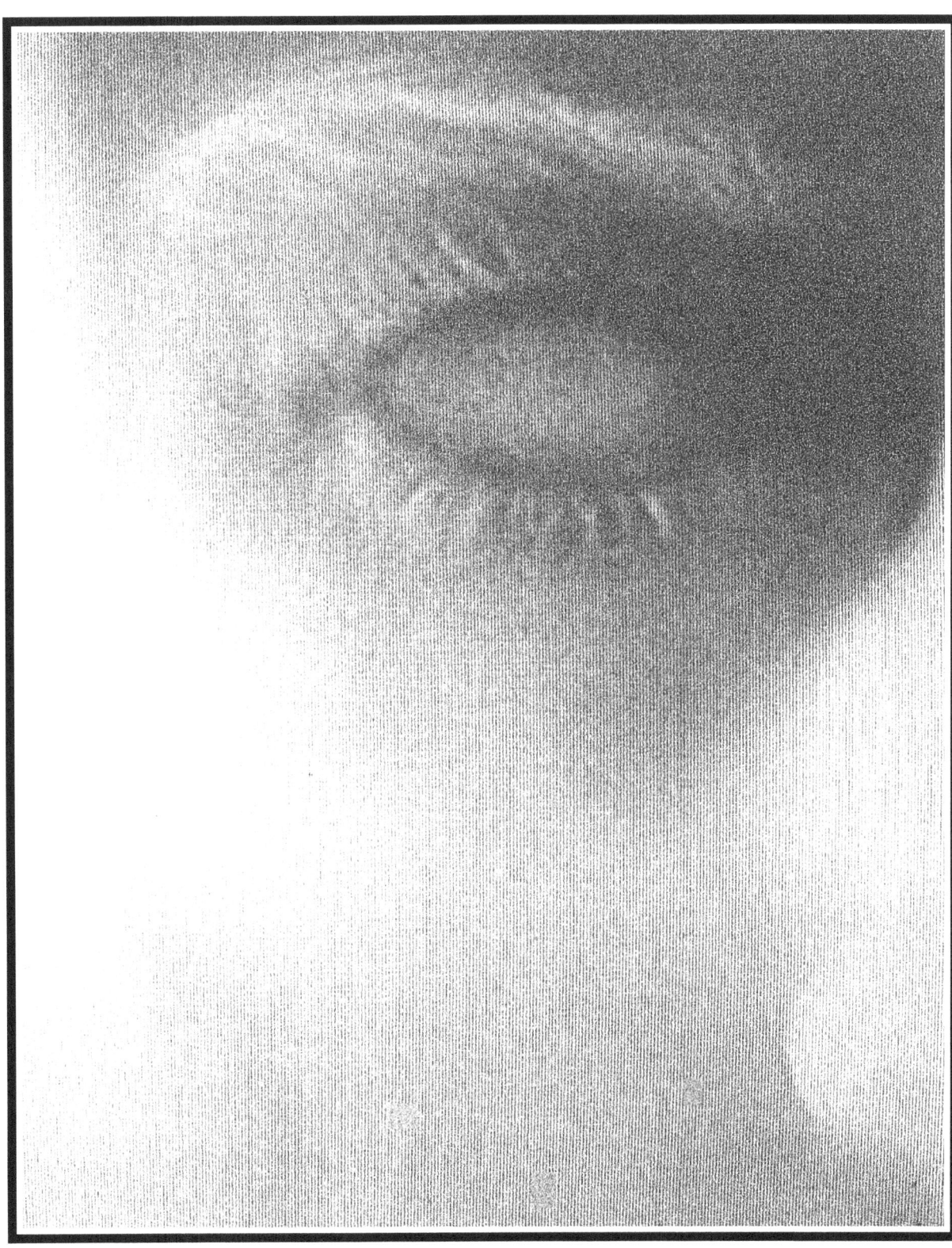

Helen Maringer

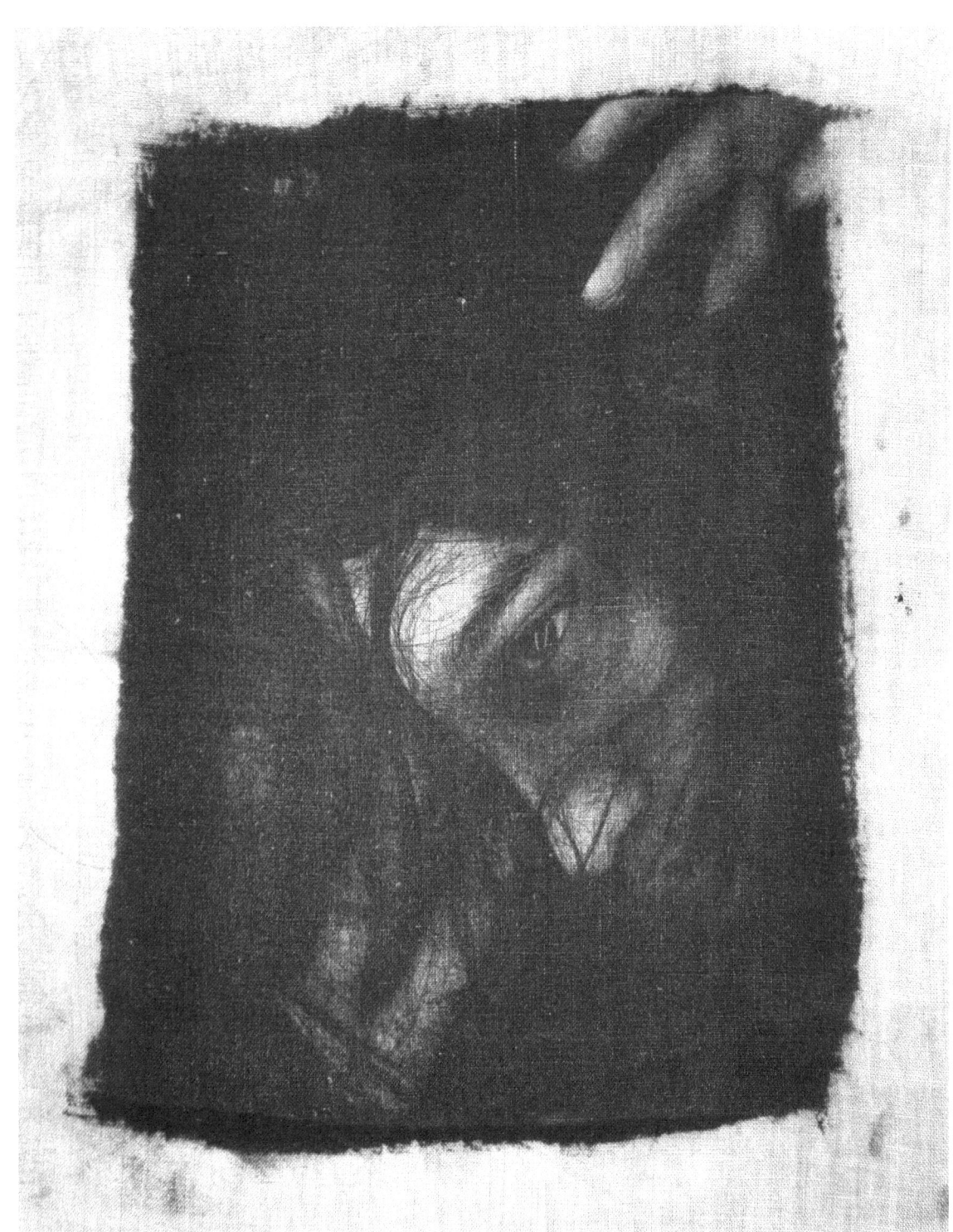

Gabriella Marks

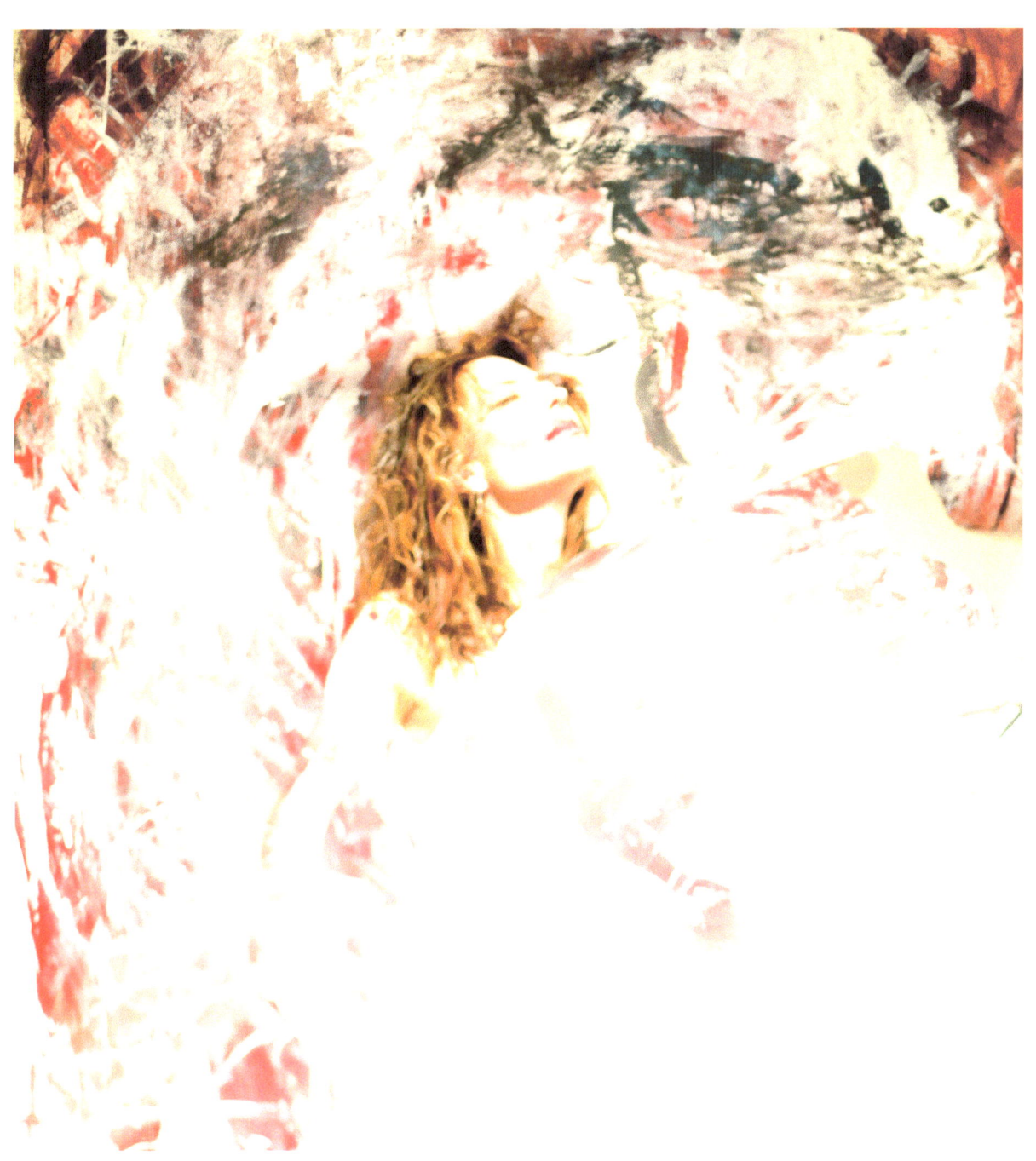

Elliott McDowell

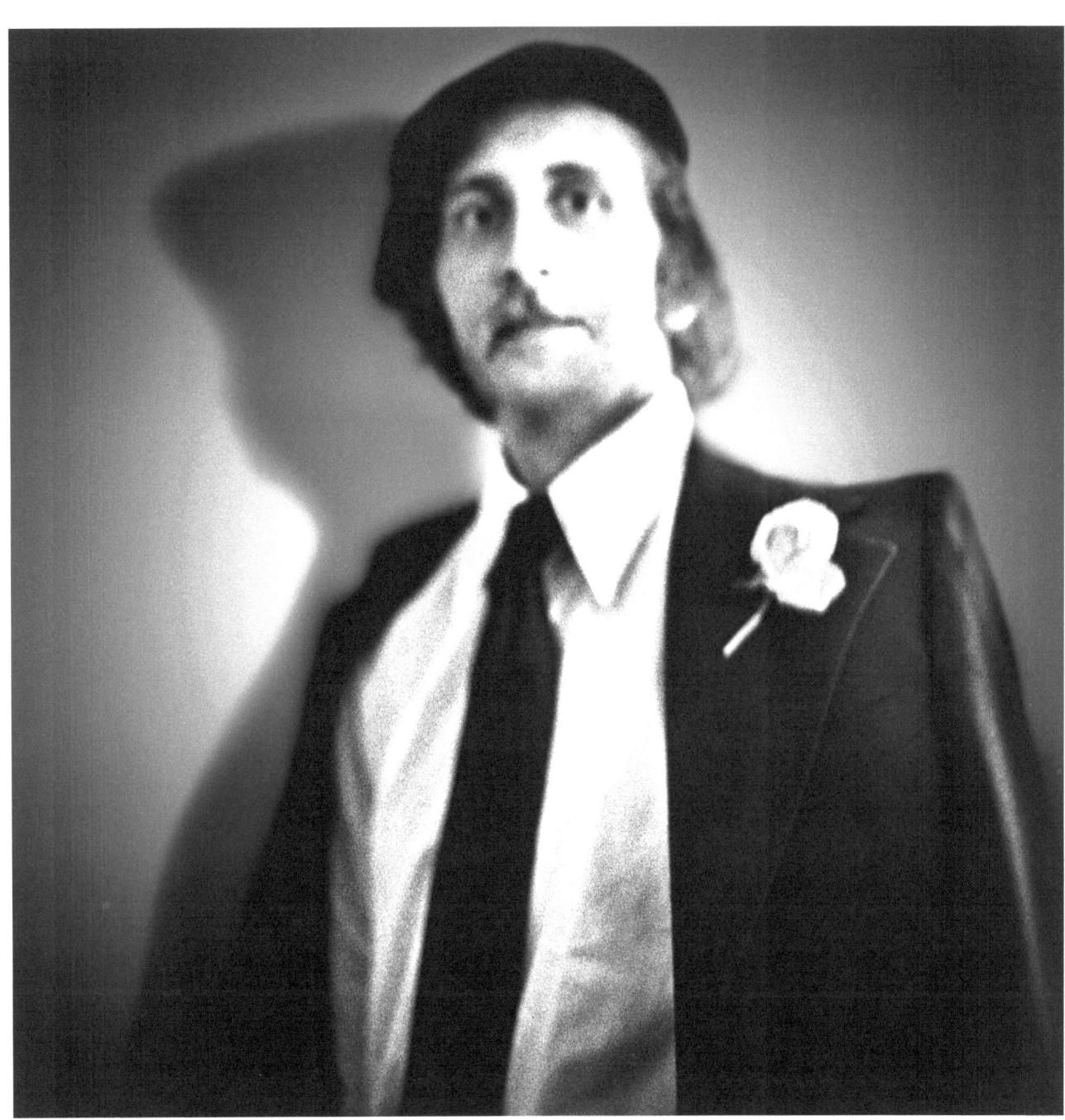

Nick Merrick

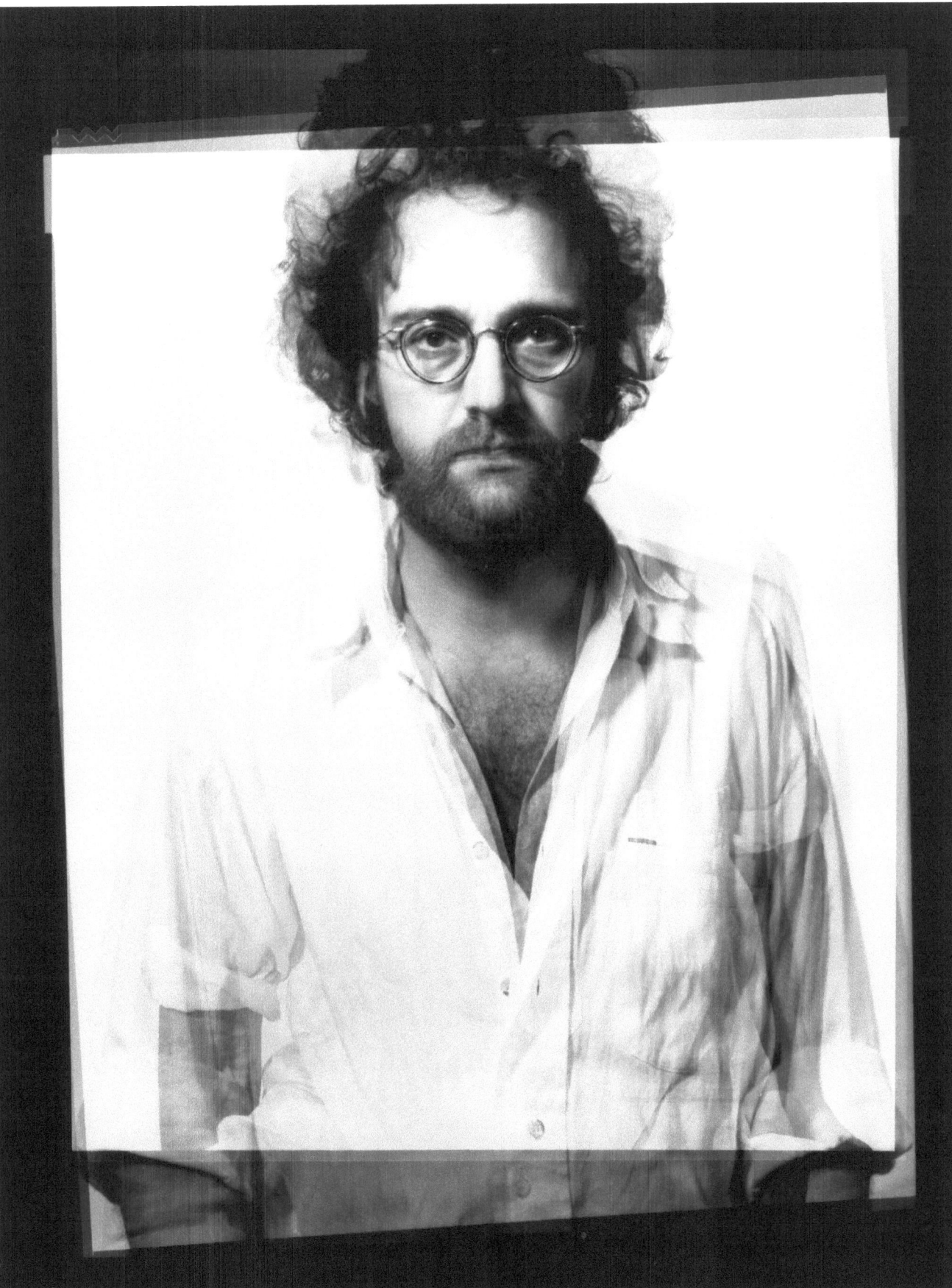

Philip Metcalf

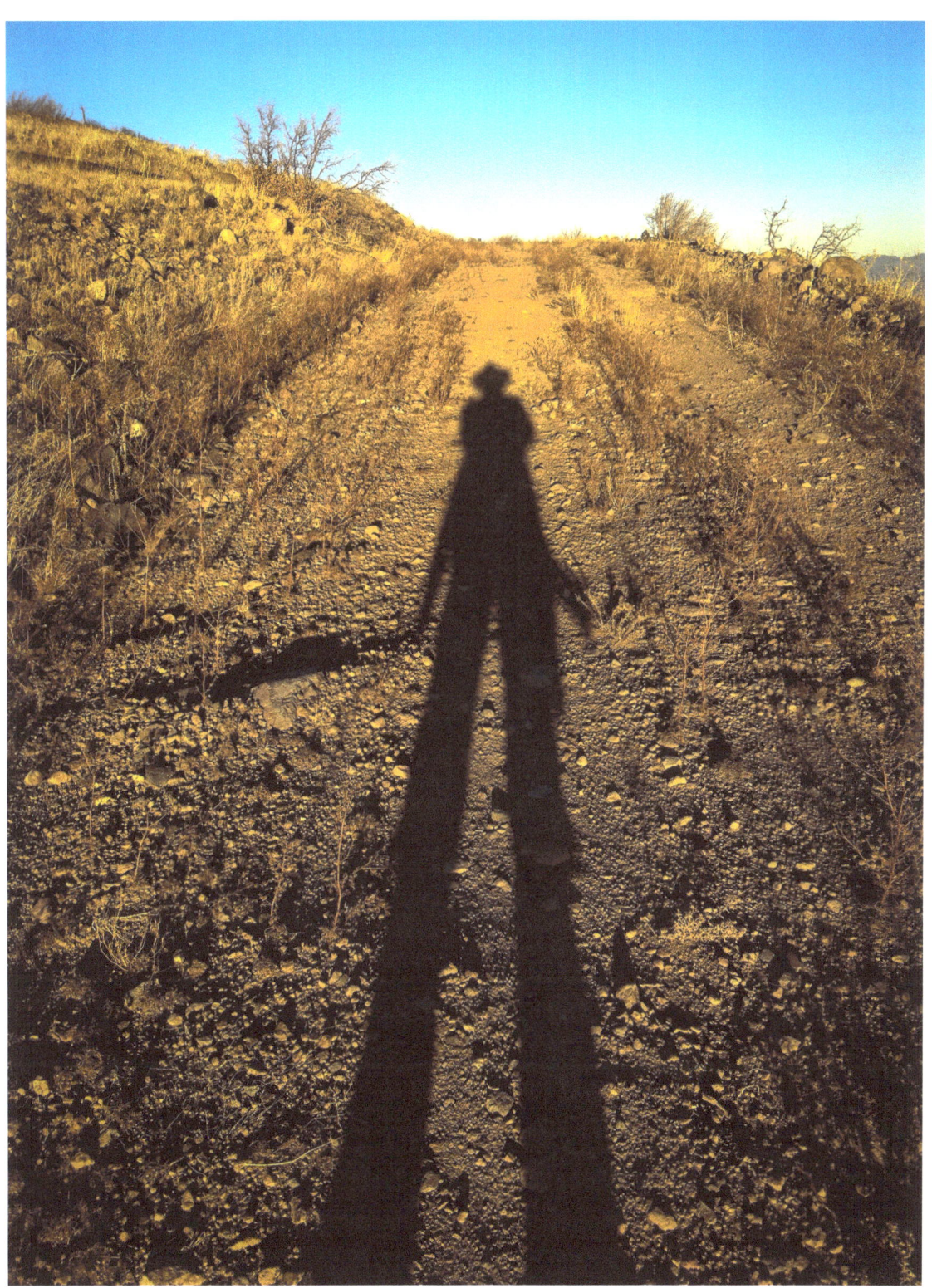

Lia Moldovan

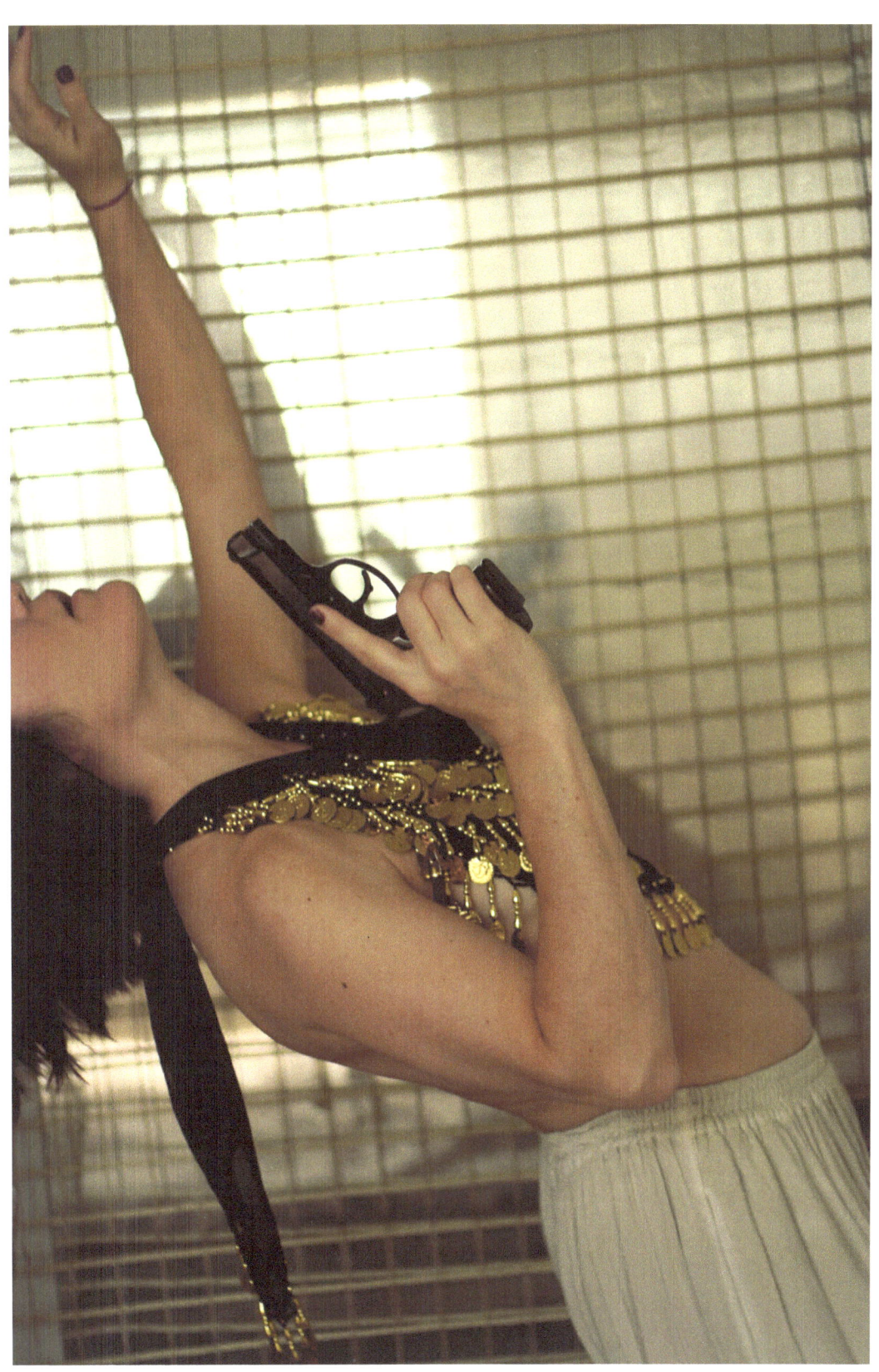

Duane Monczewski

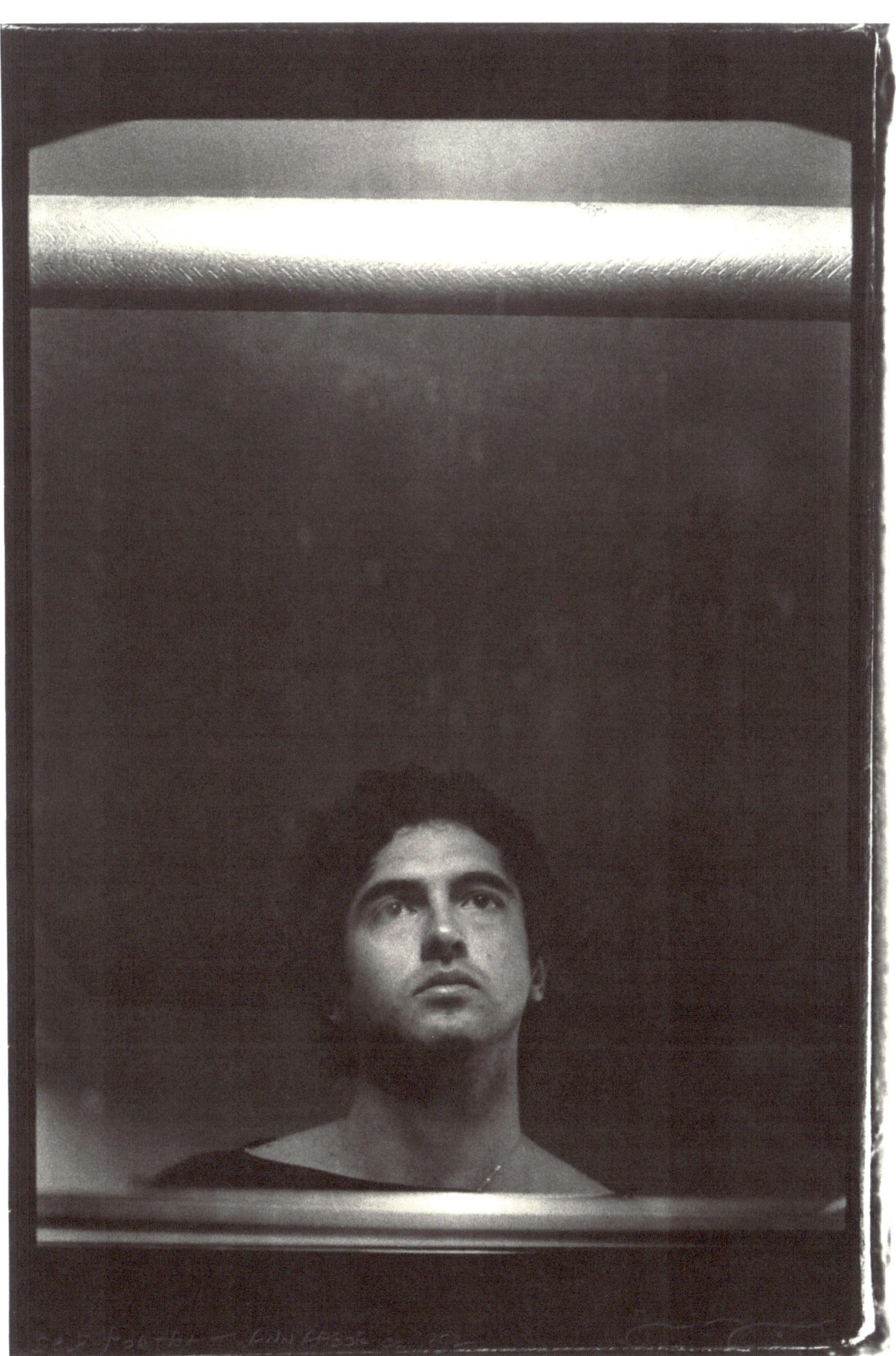

Delilah Montoya

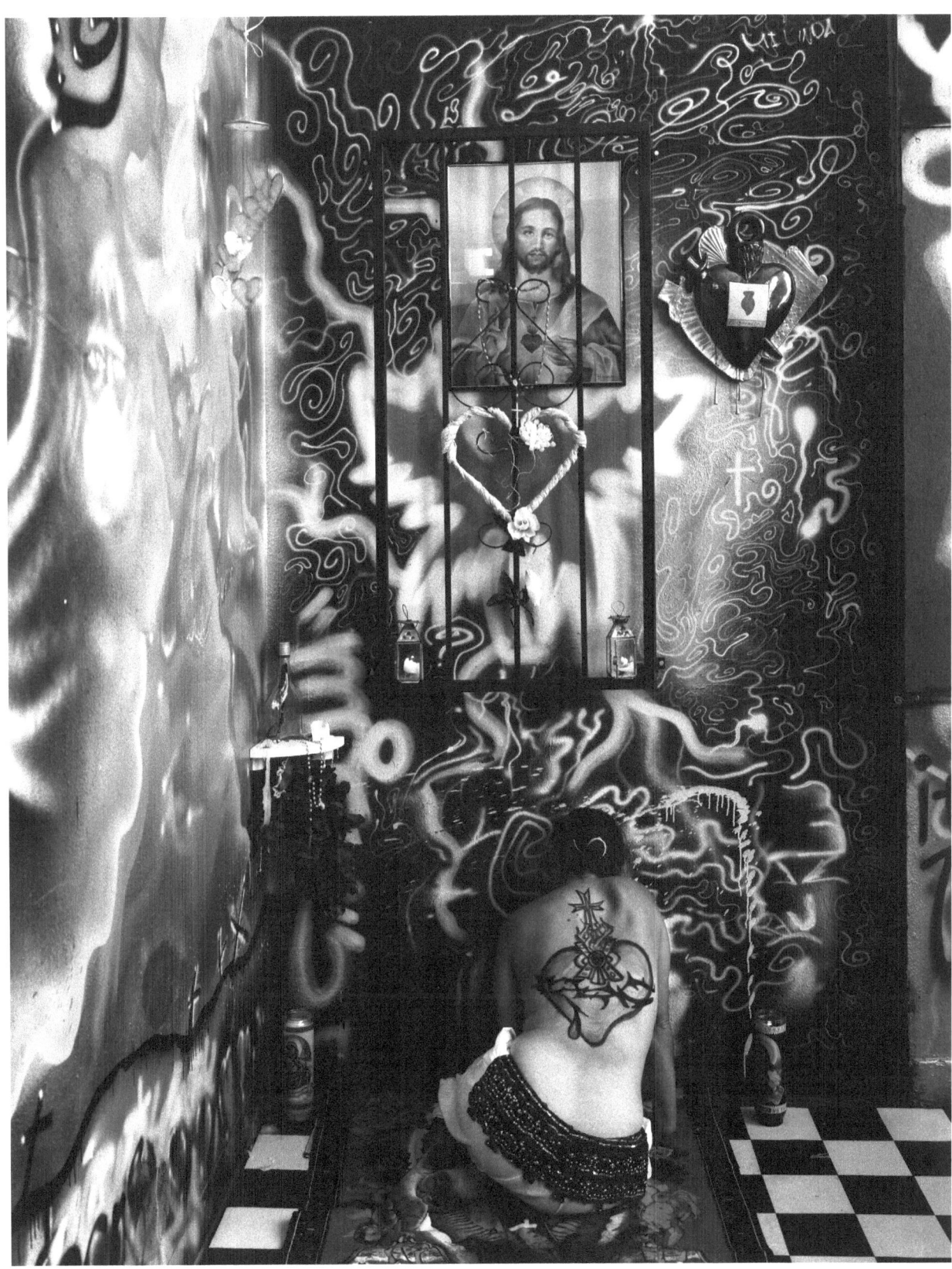

Sarah Moore

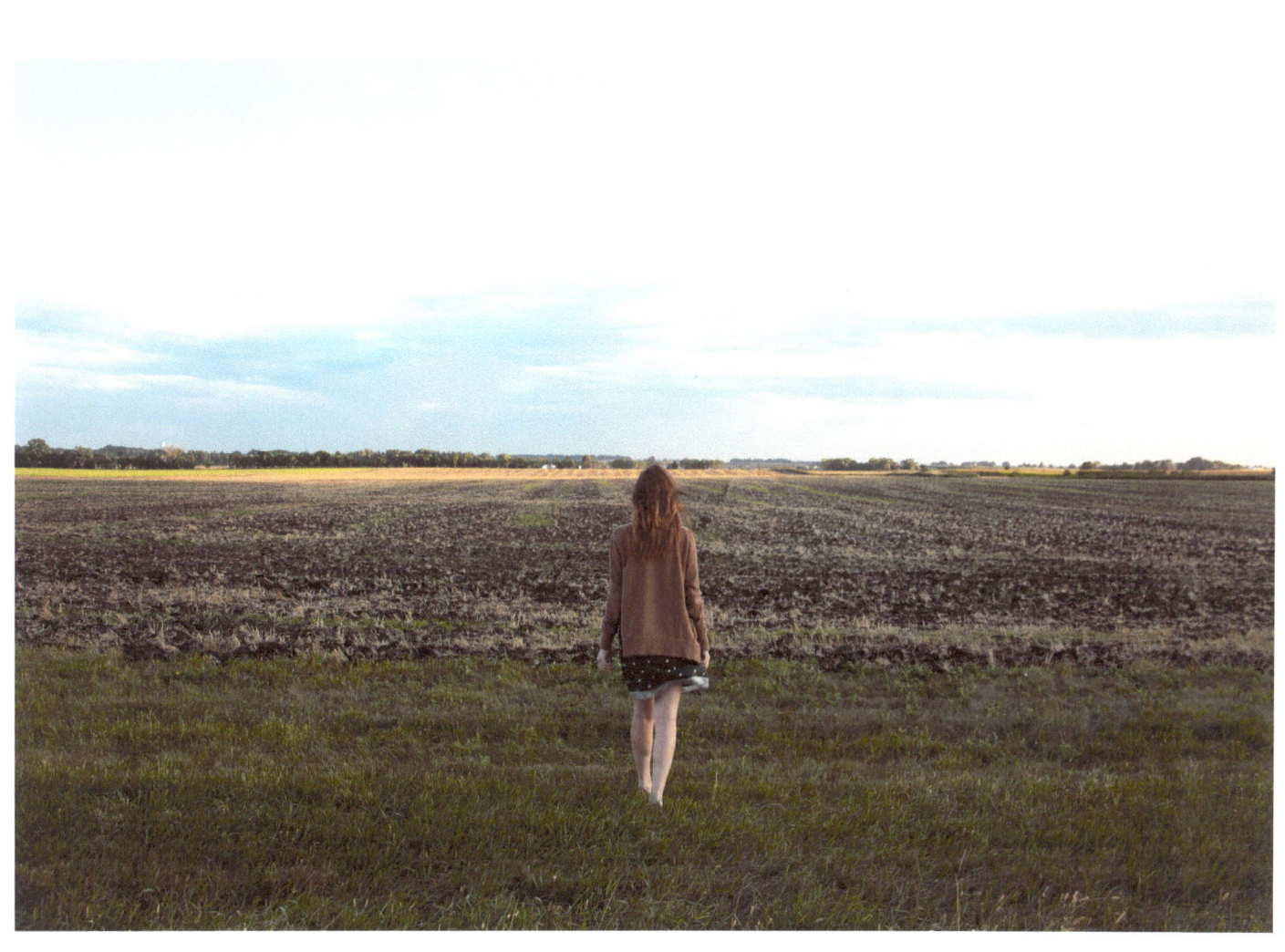

Jonathan Morse

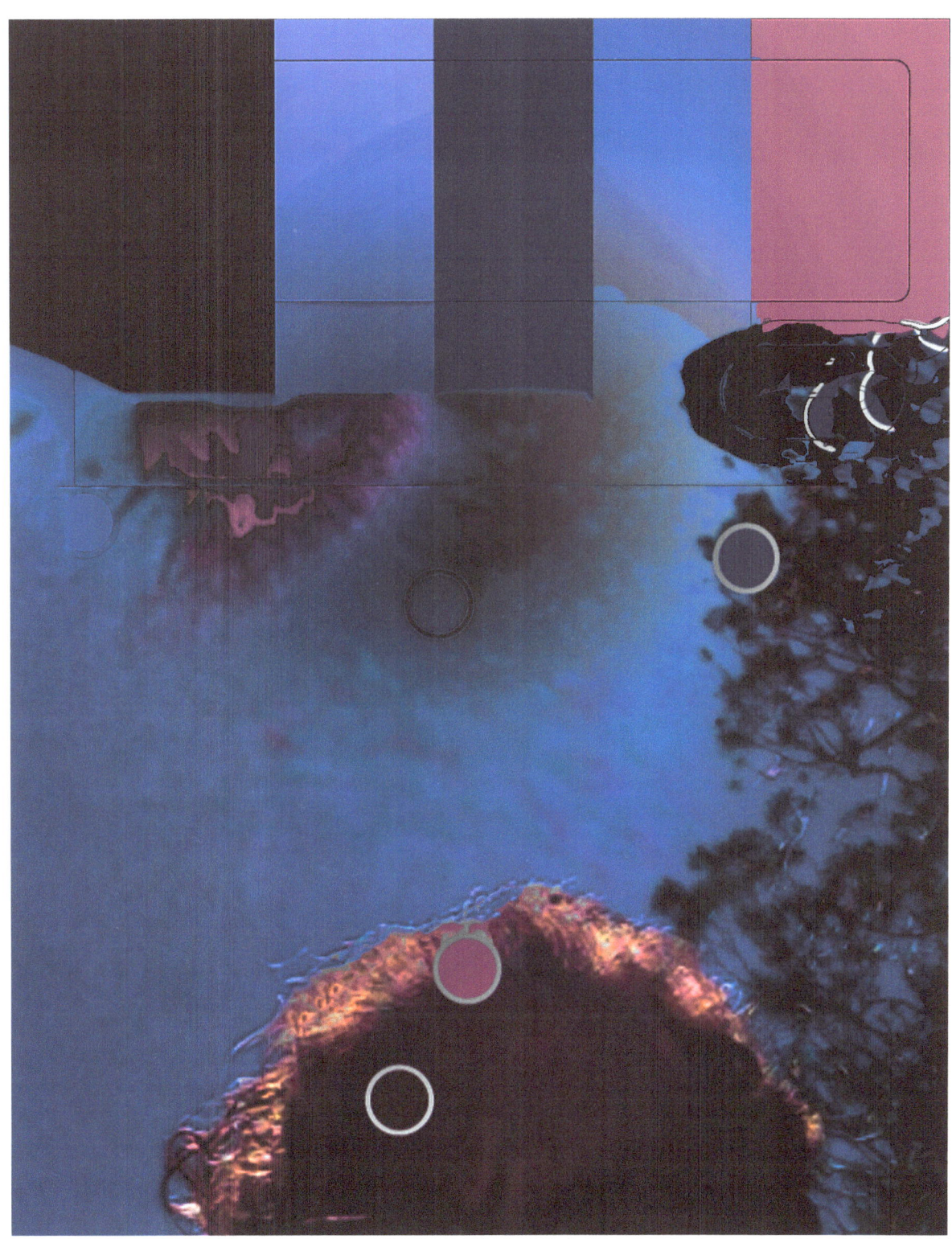

Joseph Mougel

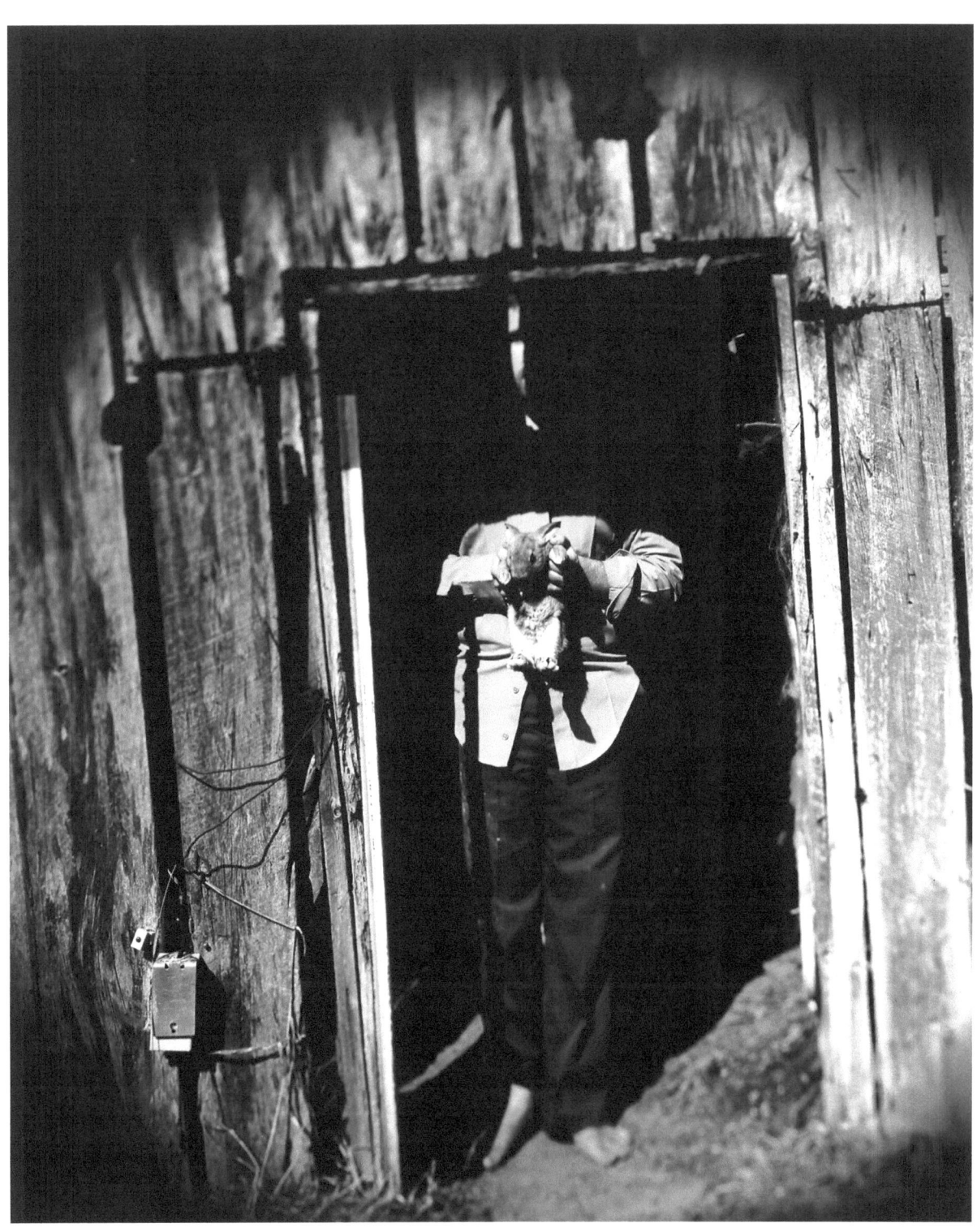

Teresa Neptune

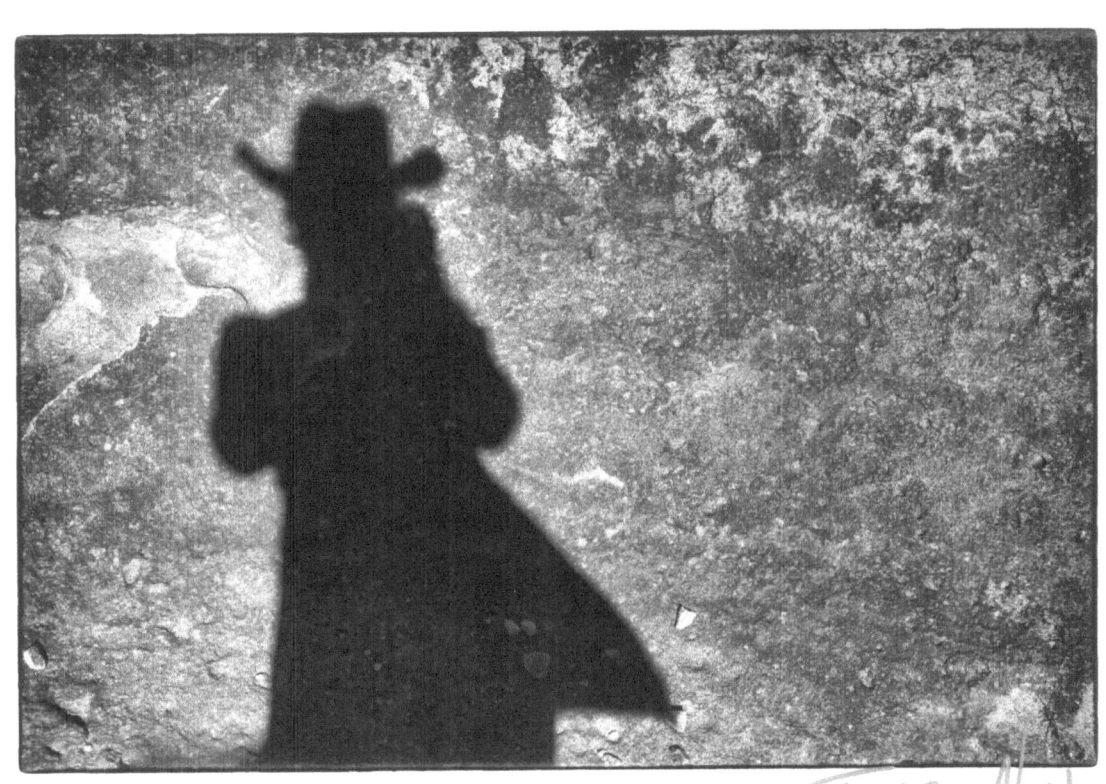

2013   Teresa Nigrin

The photographer on a windy day
City of Rocks, New Mexico, 2006

Nic Nicosia

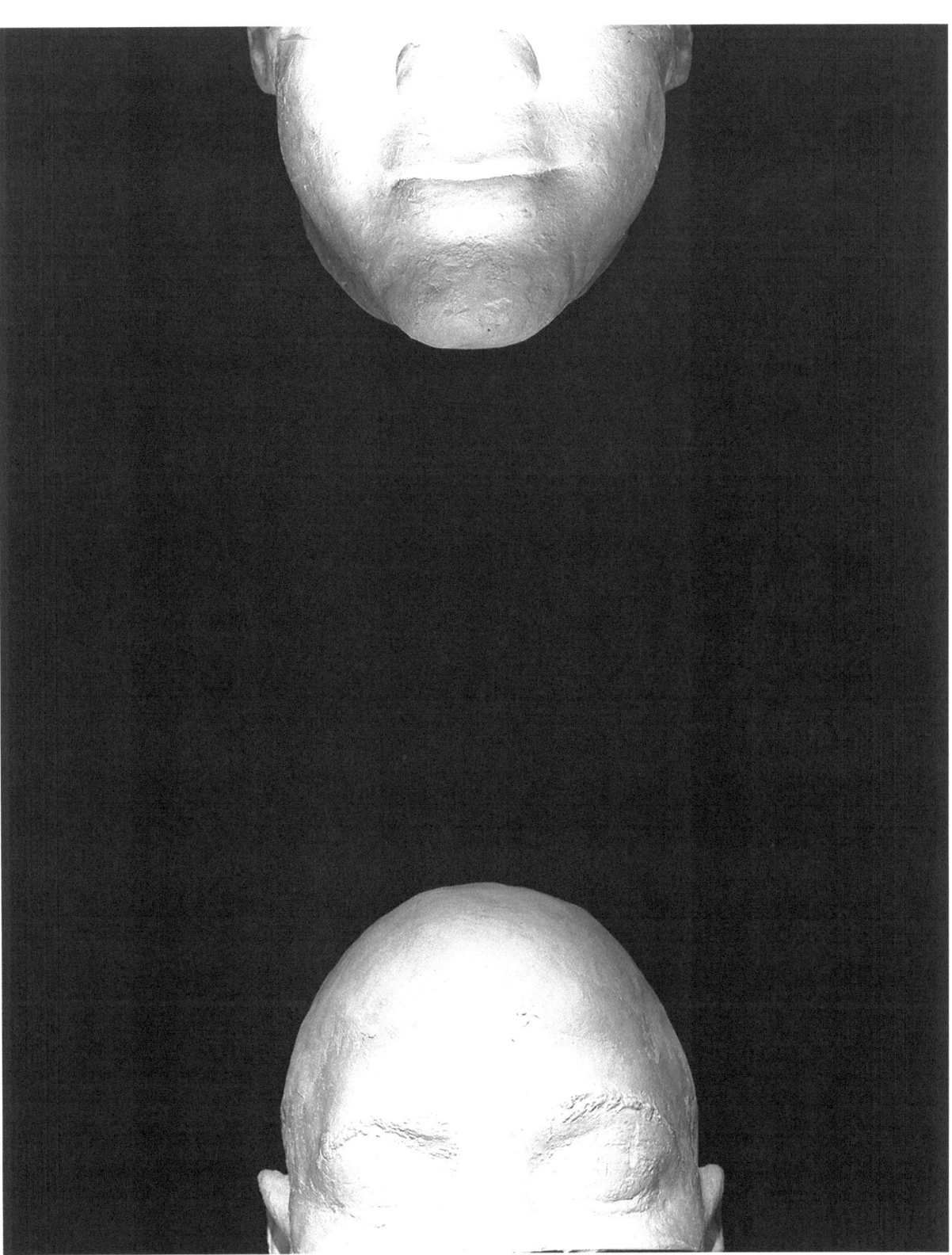

Clay Peres

REASON #33 THERE IS NO ST. PERES

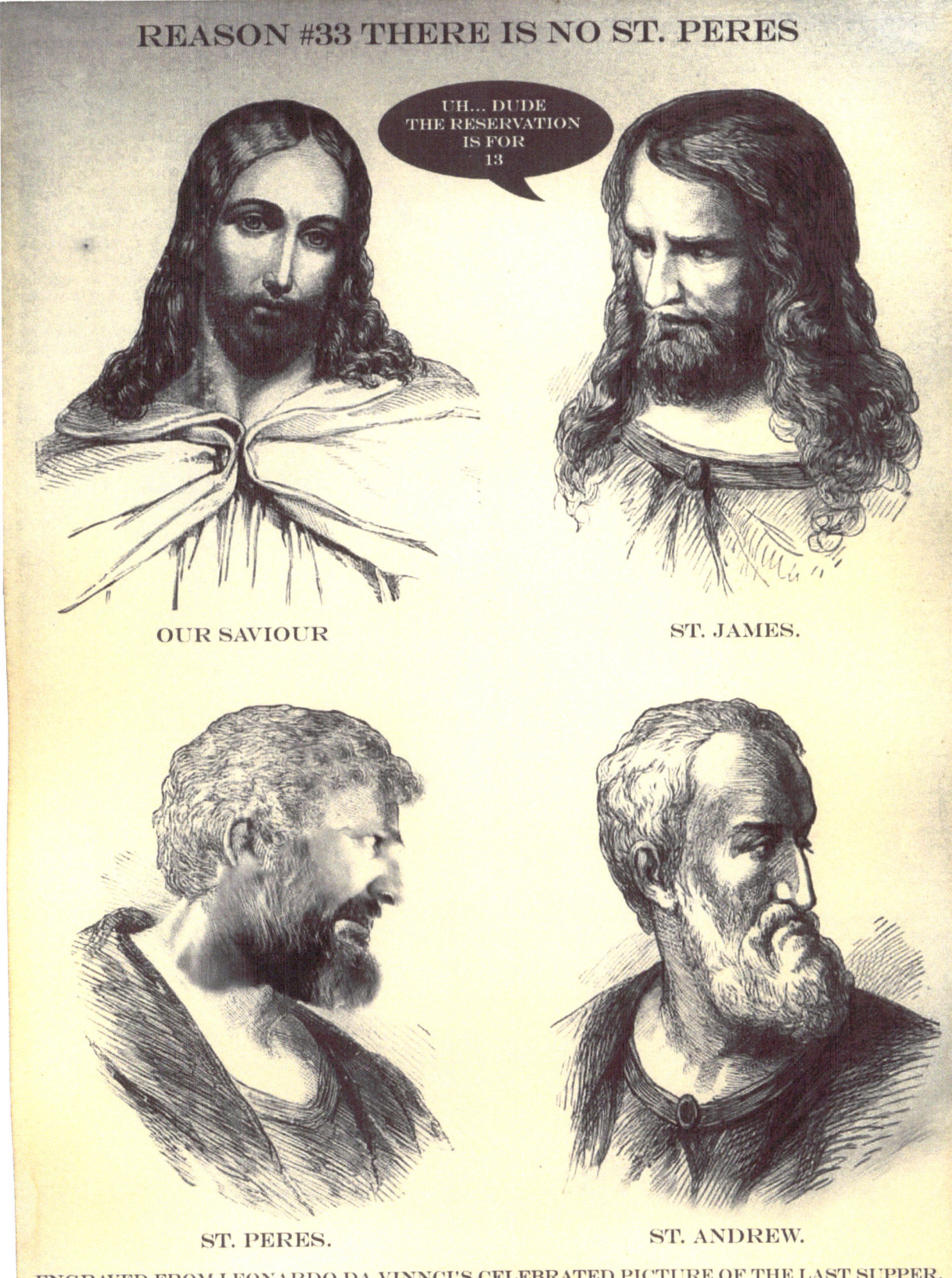

ENGRAVED FROM LEONARDO DA VINNCI'S CELEBRATED PICTURE OF THE LAST SUPPER.

Jane Phillips

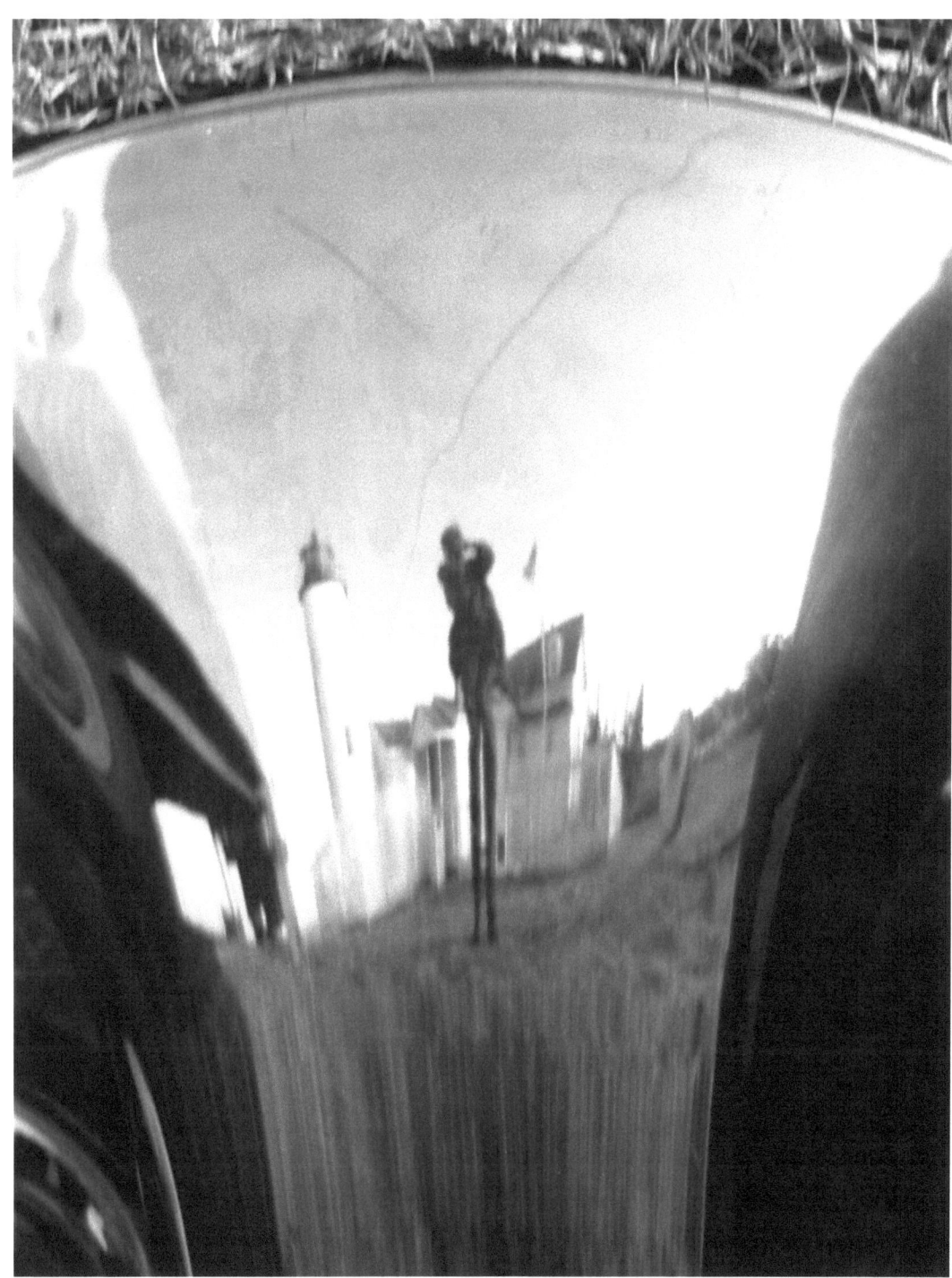

Daniel Quat

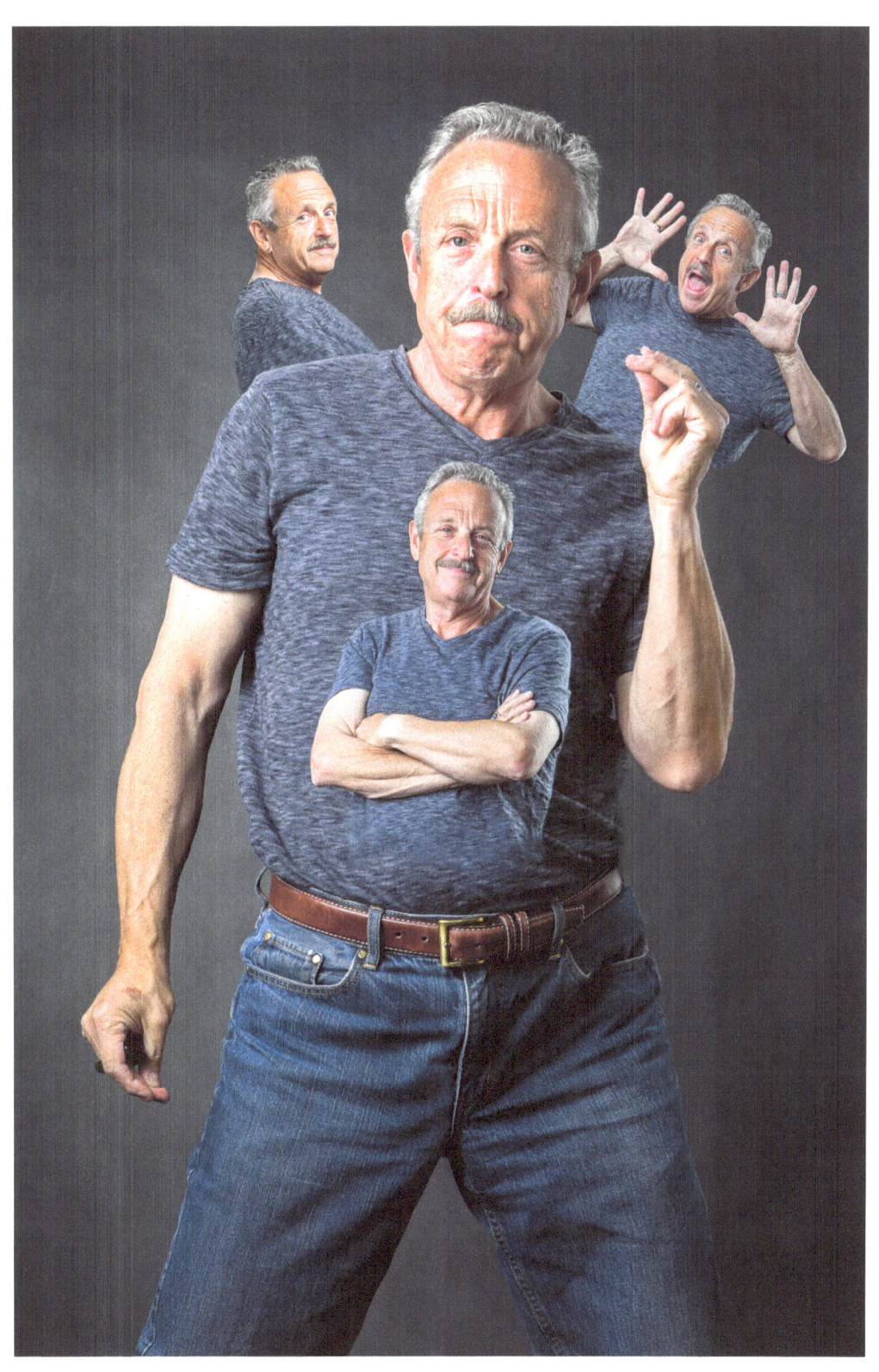

Dave Reichert

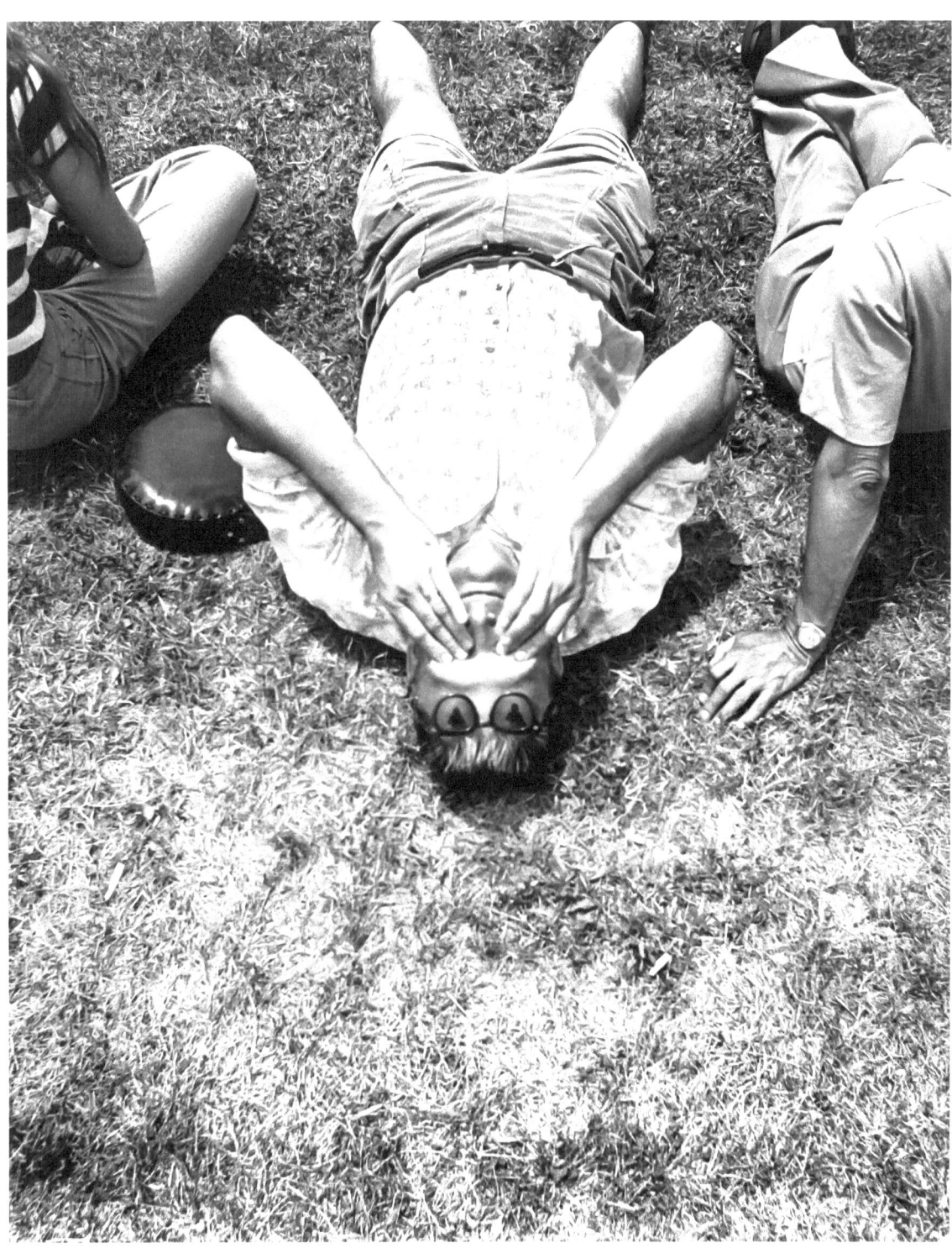

Meridel Rubenstein

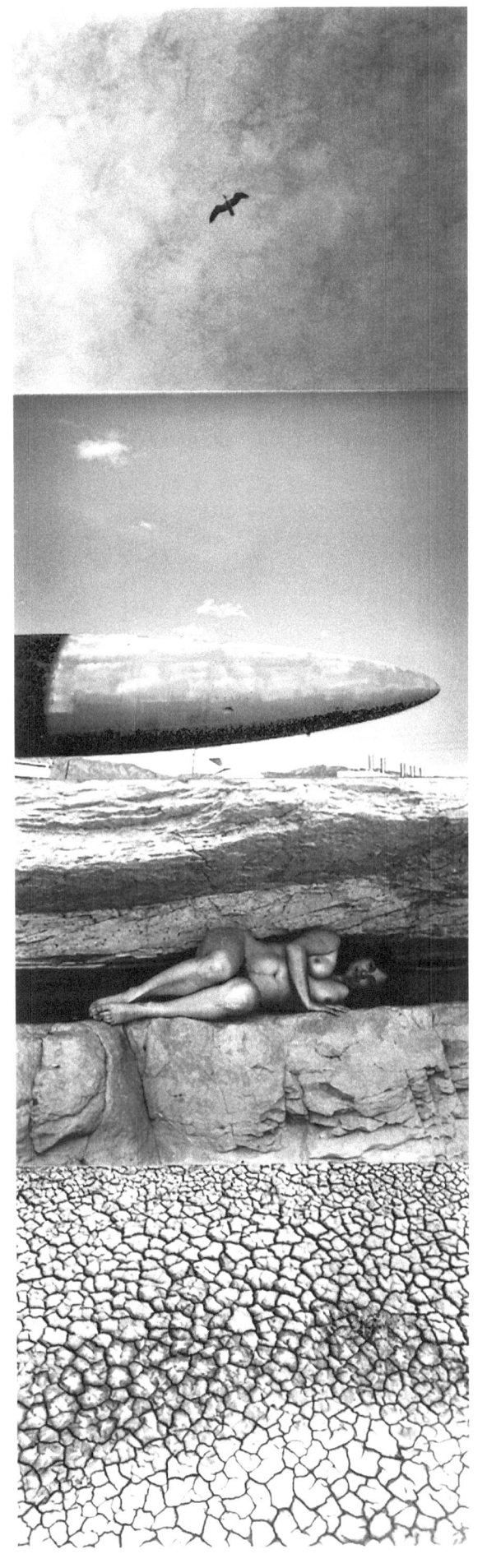

Janet Russek

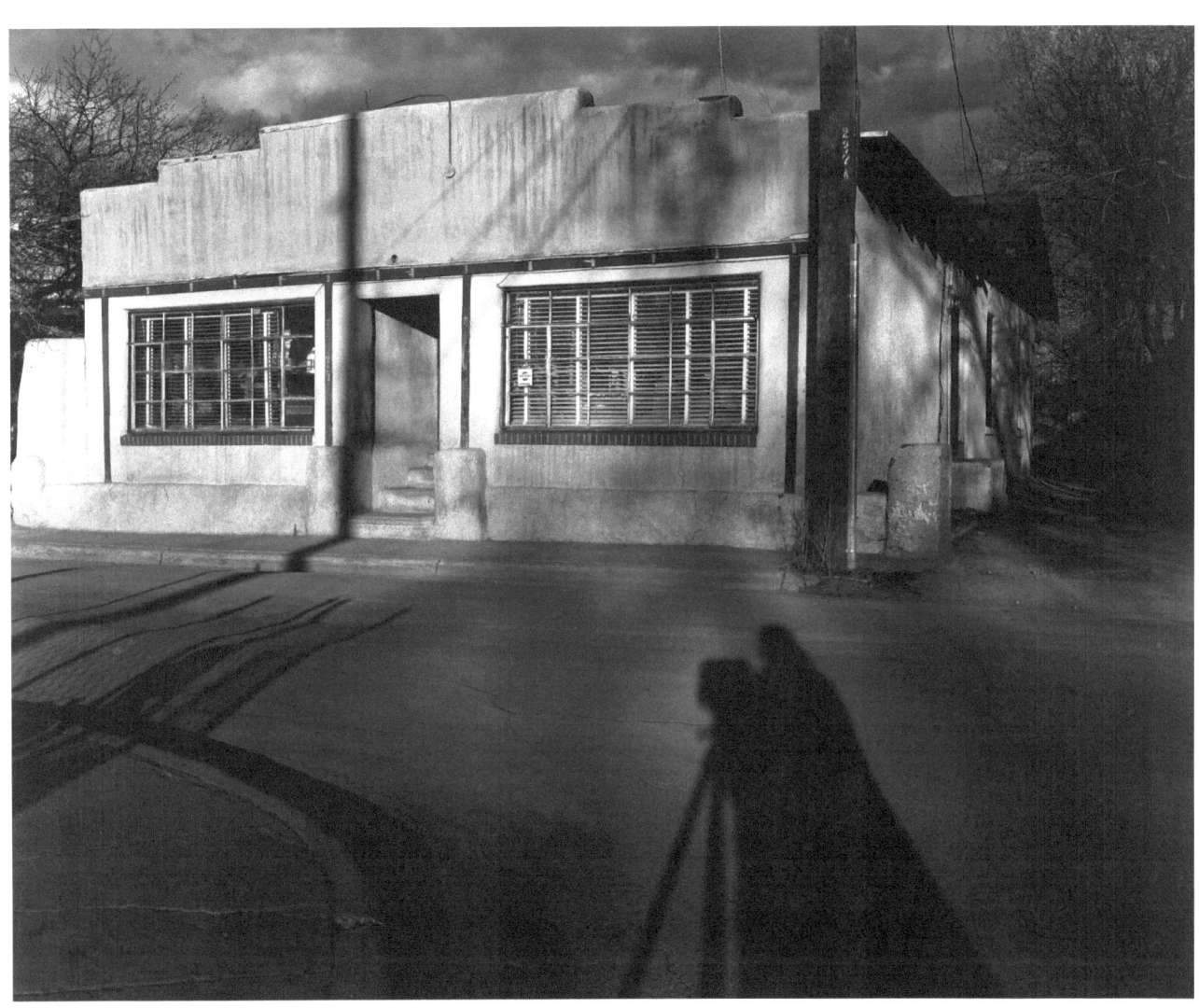

Kate Russell

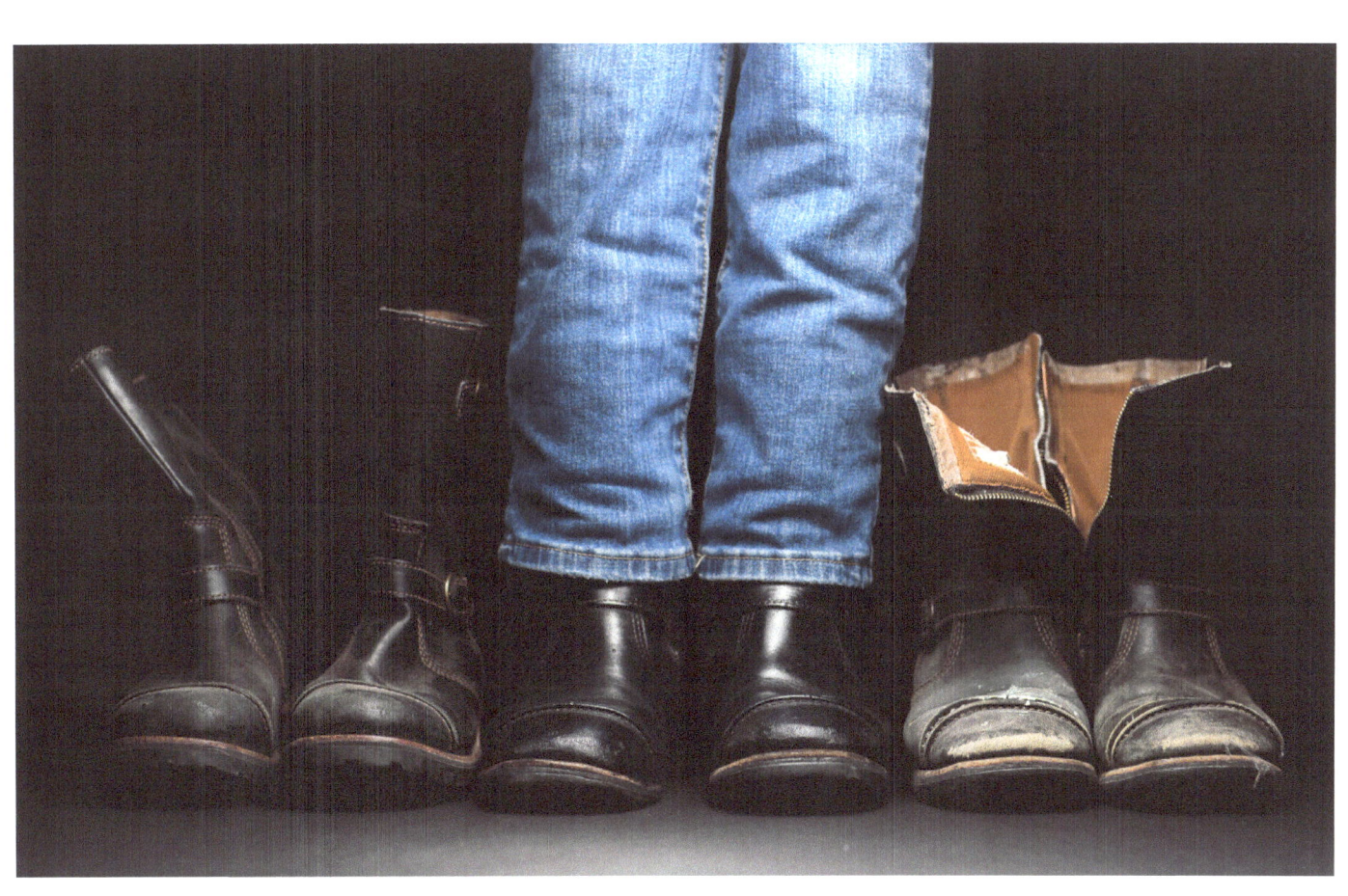

Ward Russell

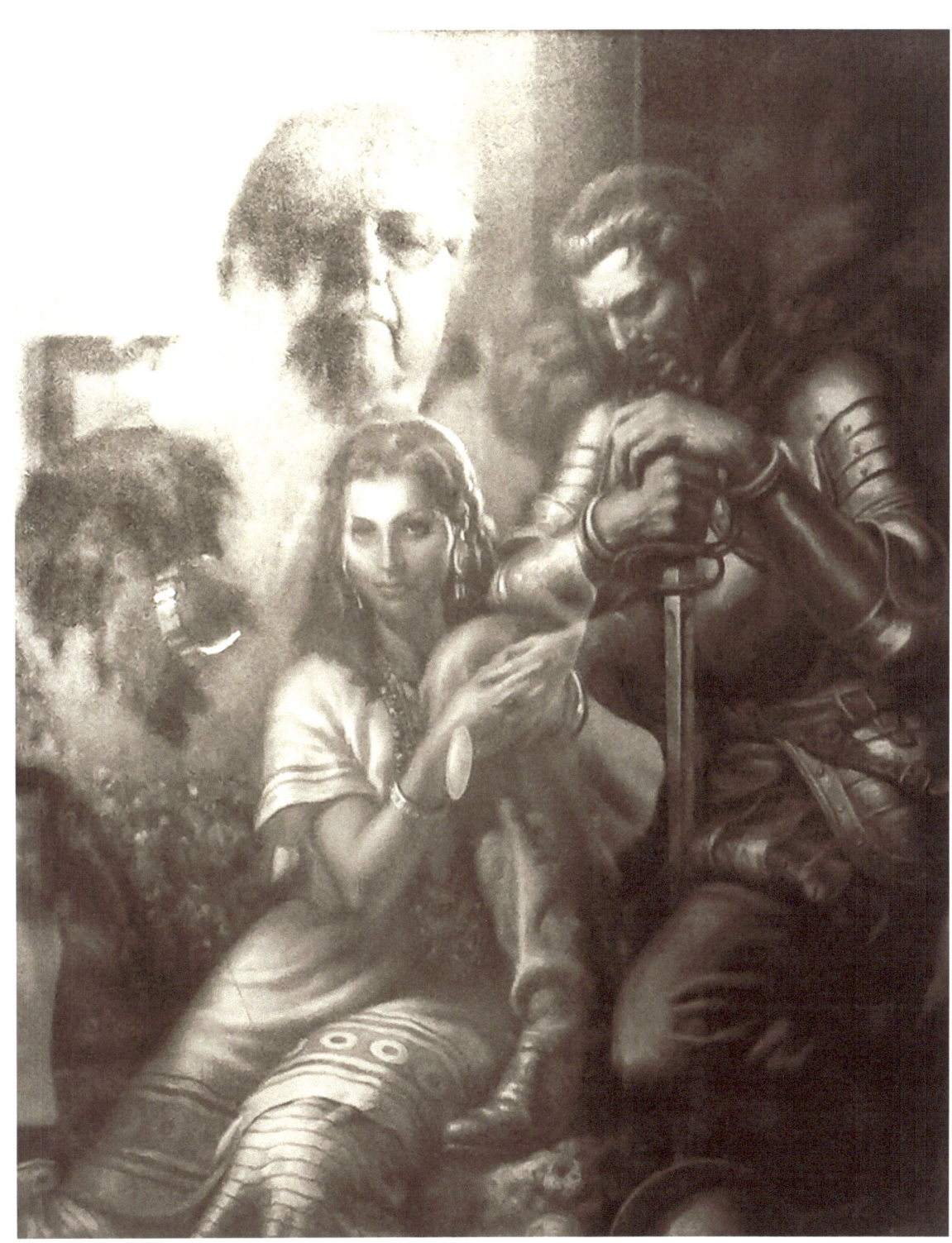

Tara Raye Russo

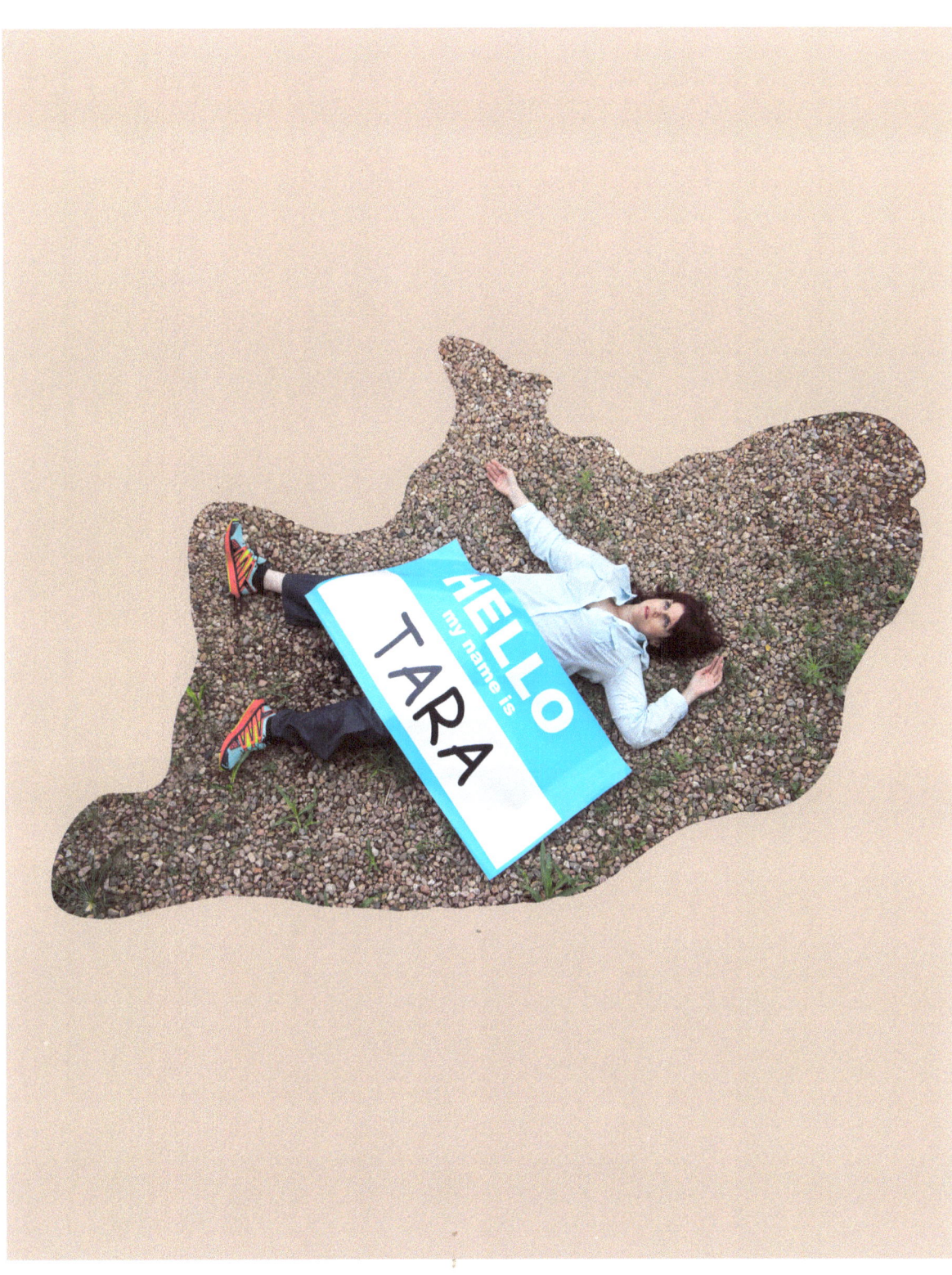

Key Sanders

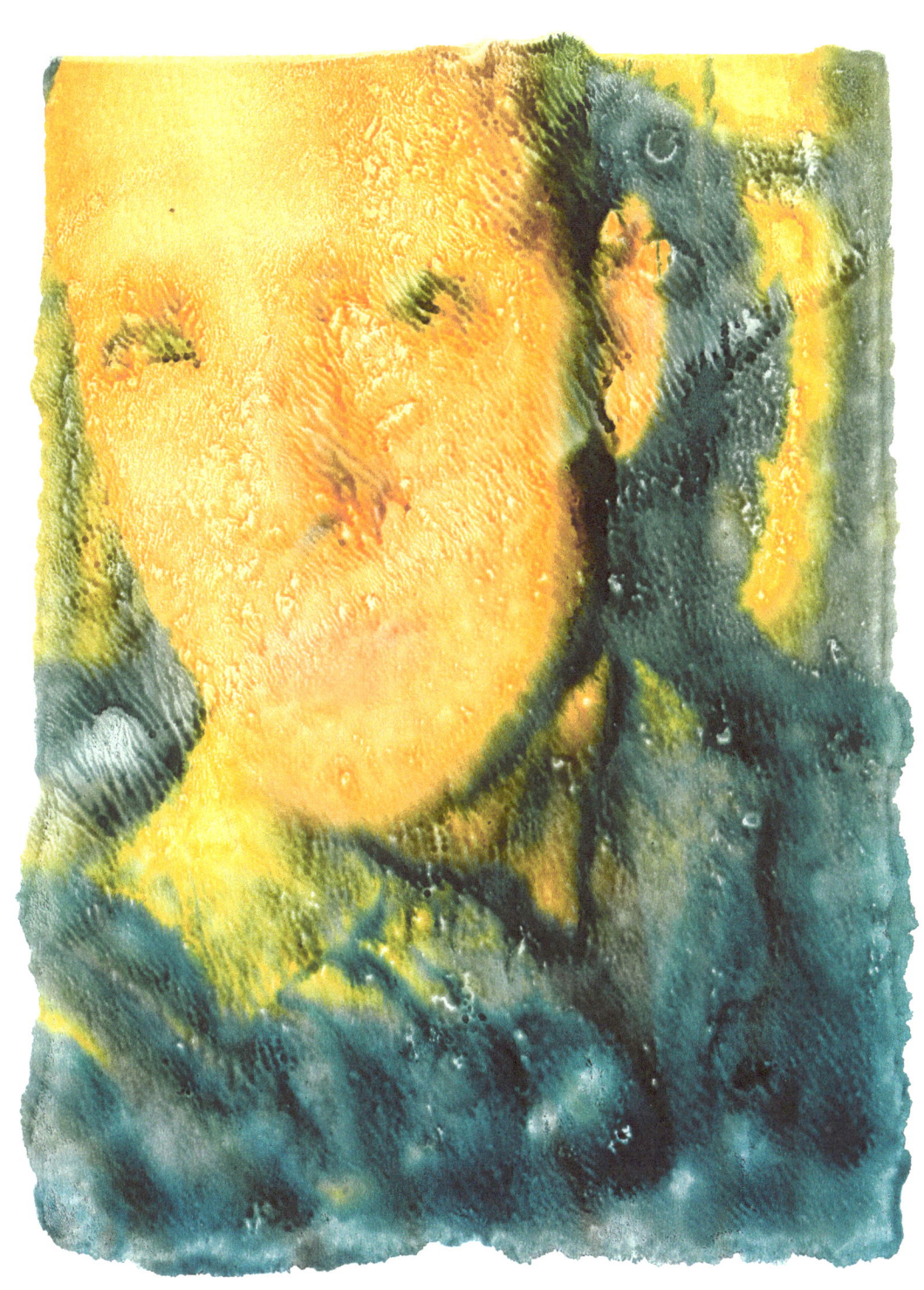

Celia Luz Santos

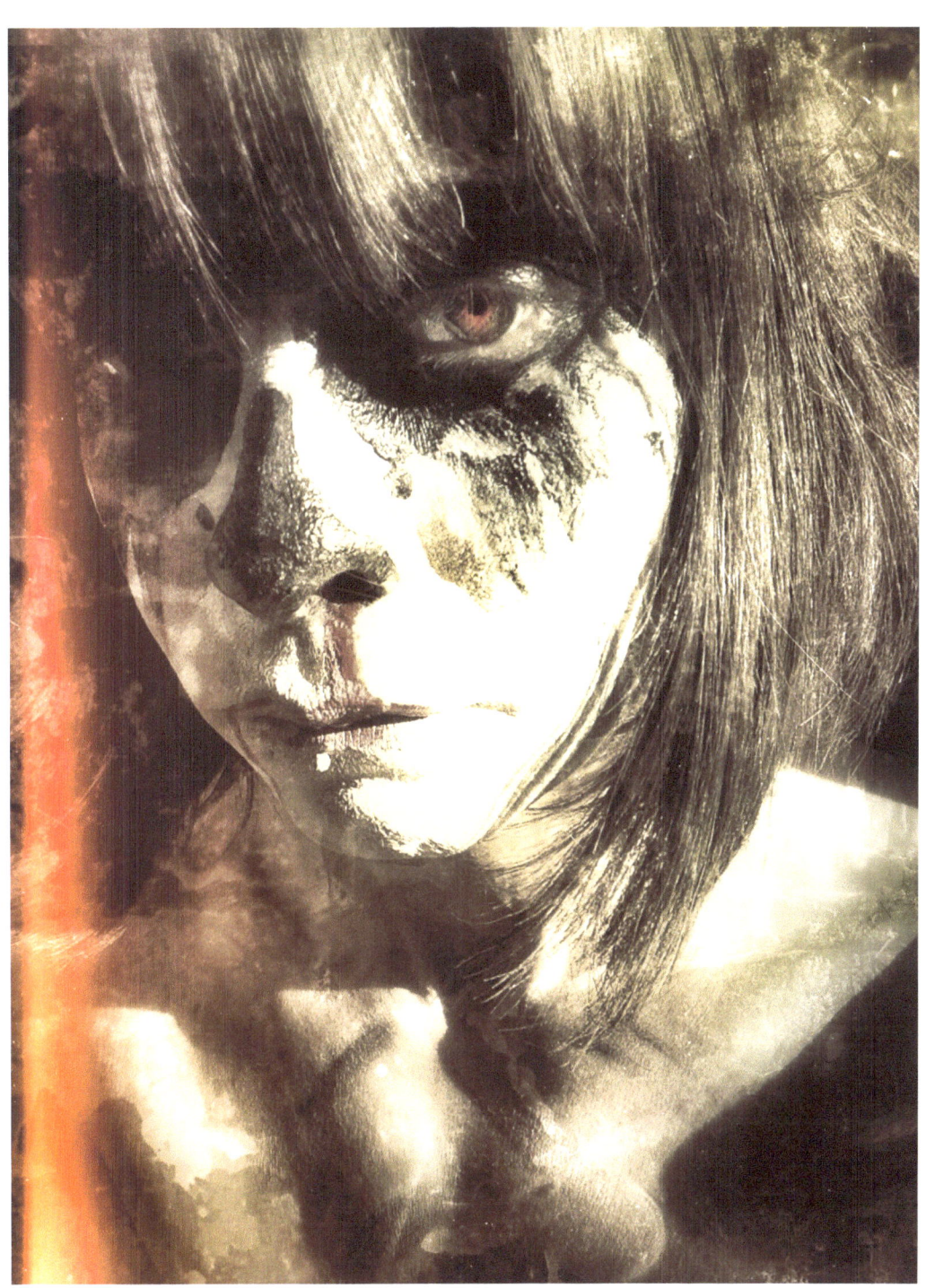

Suzanne Sbarge

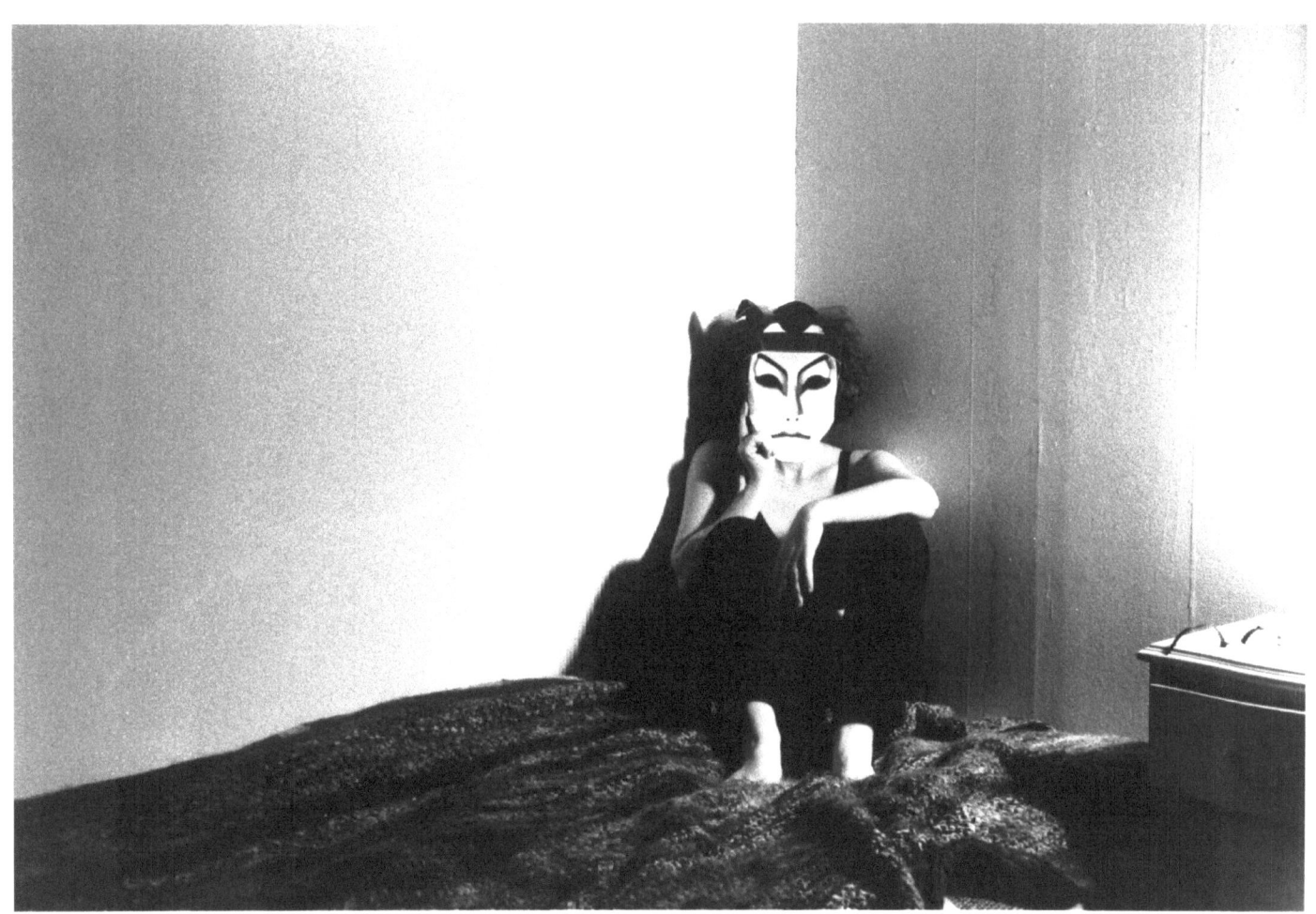

David Scheinbaum

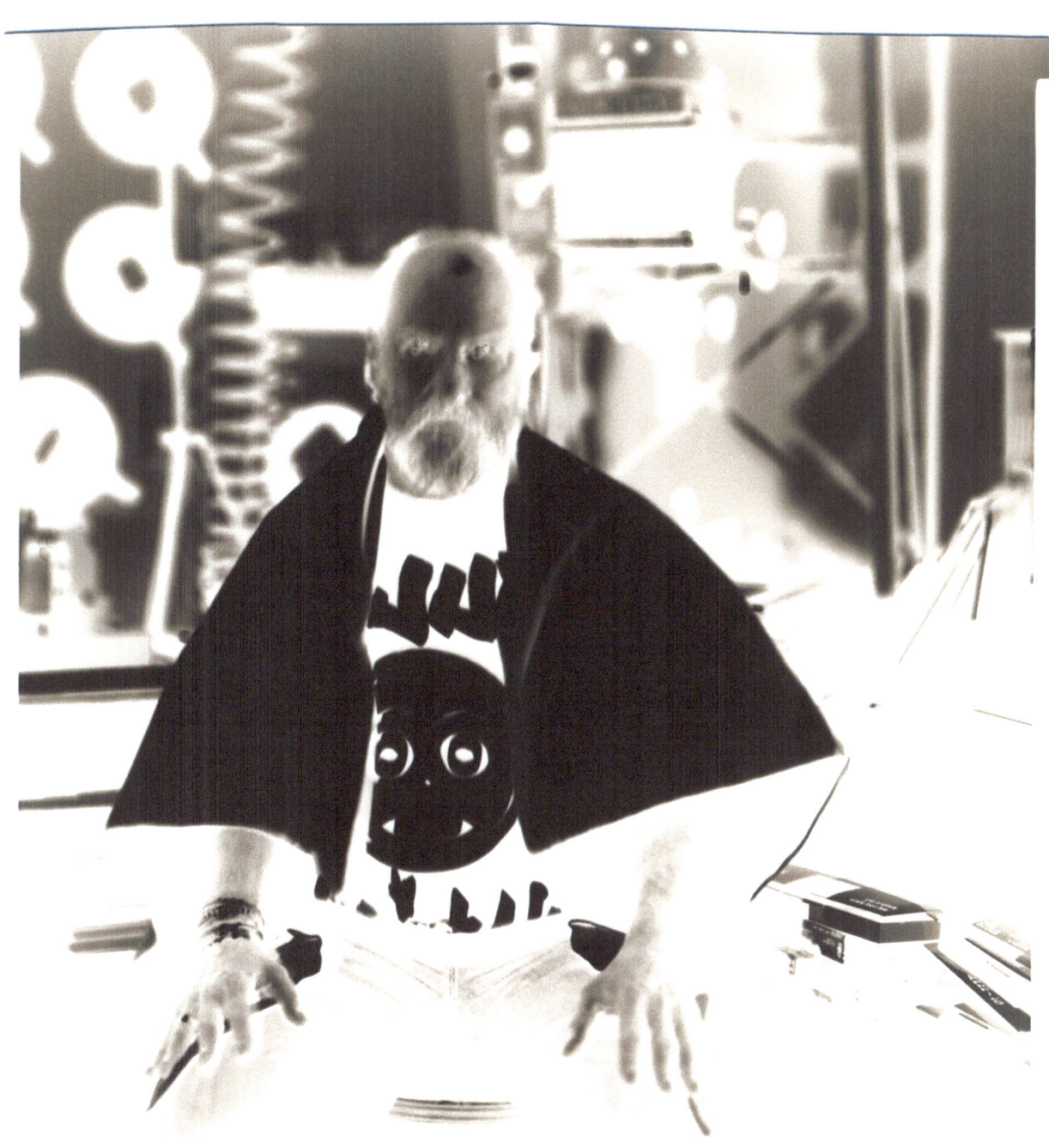

Jennifer Schlesinger Hanson

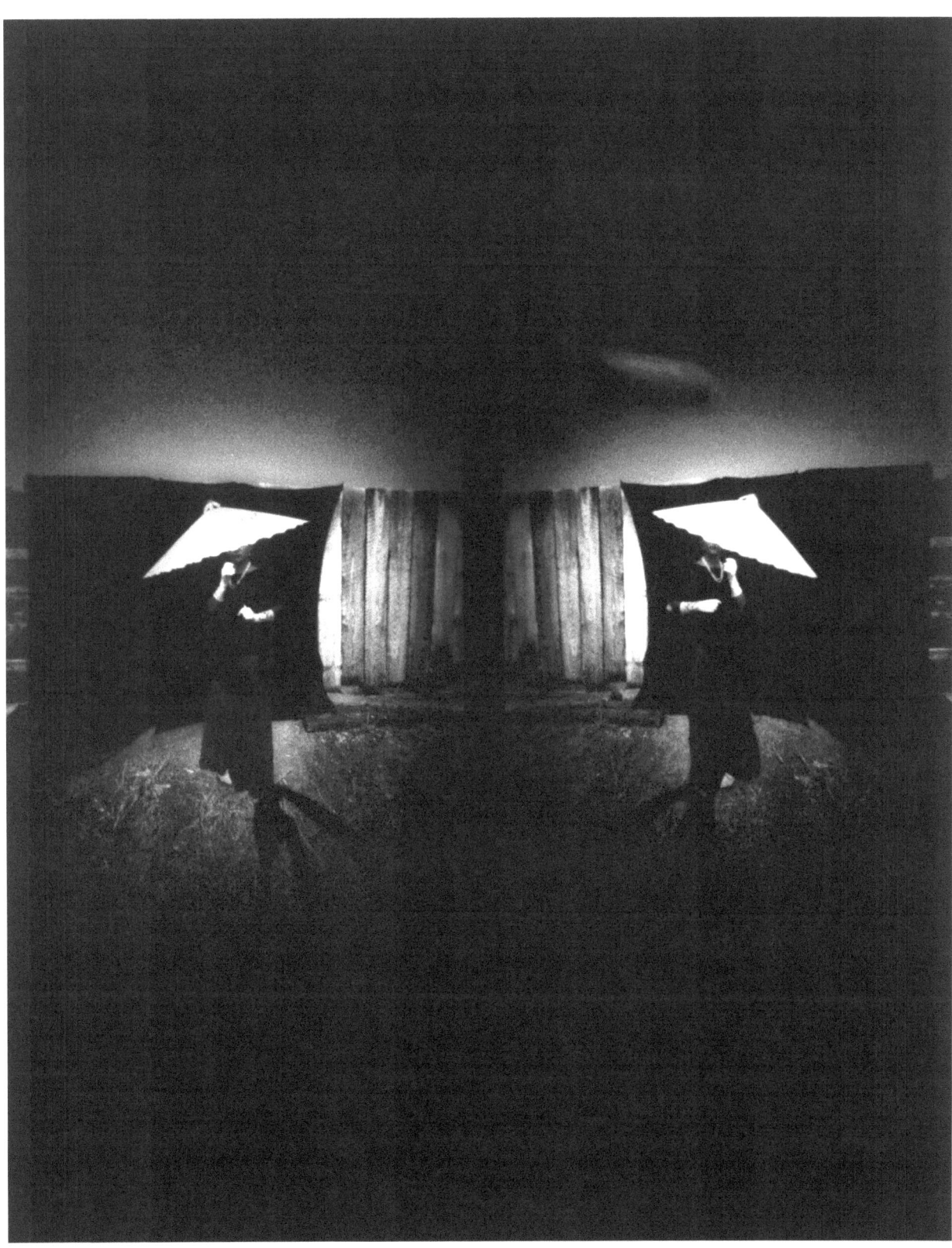

Andrea Senutovitch

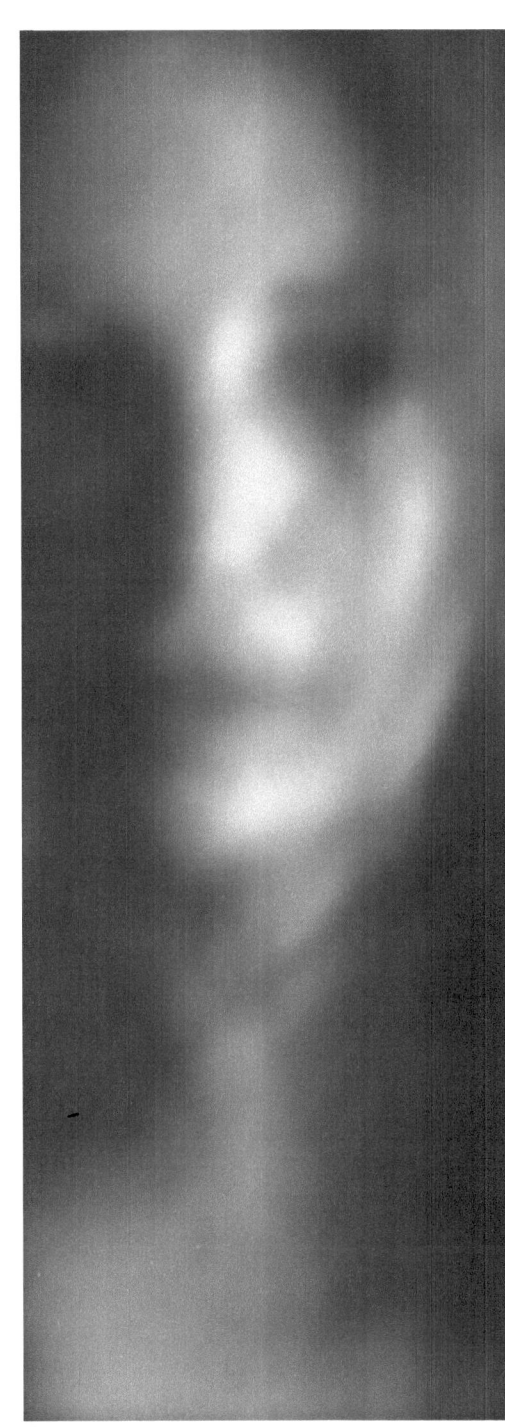

Frances Seward

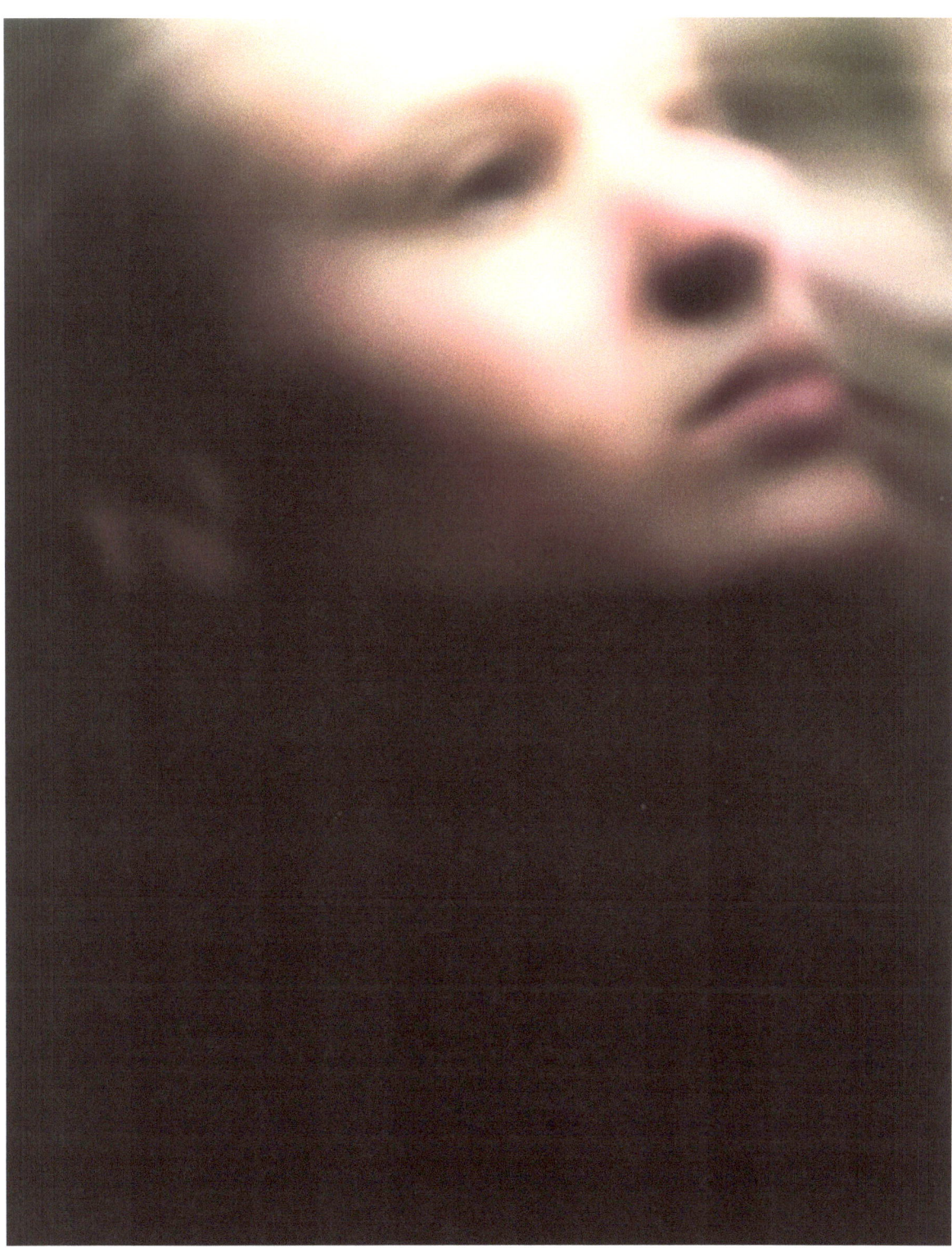

Laura Shields

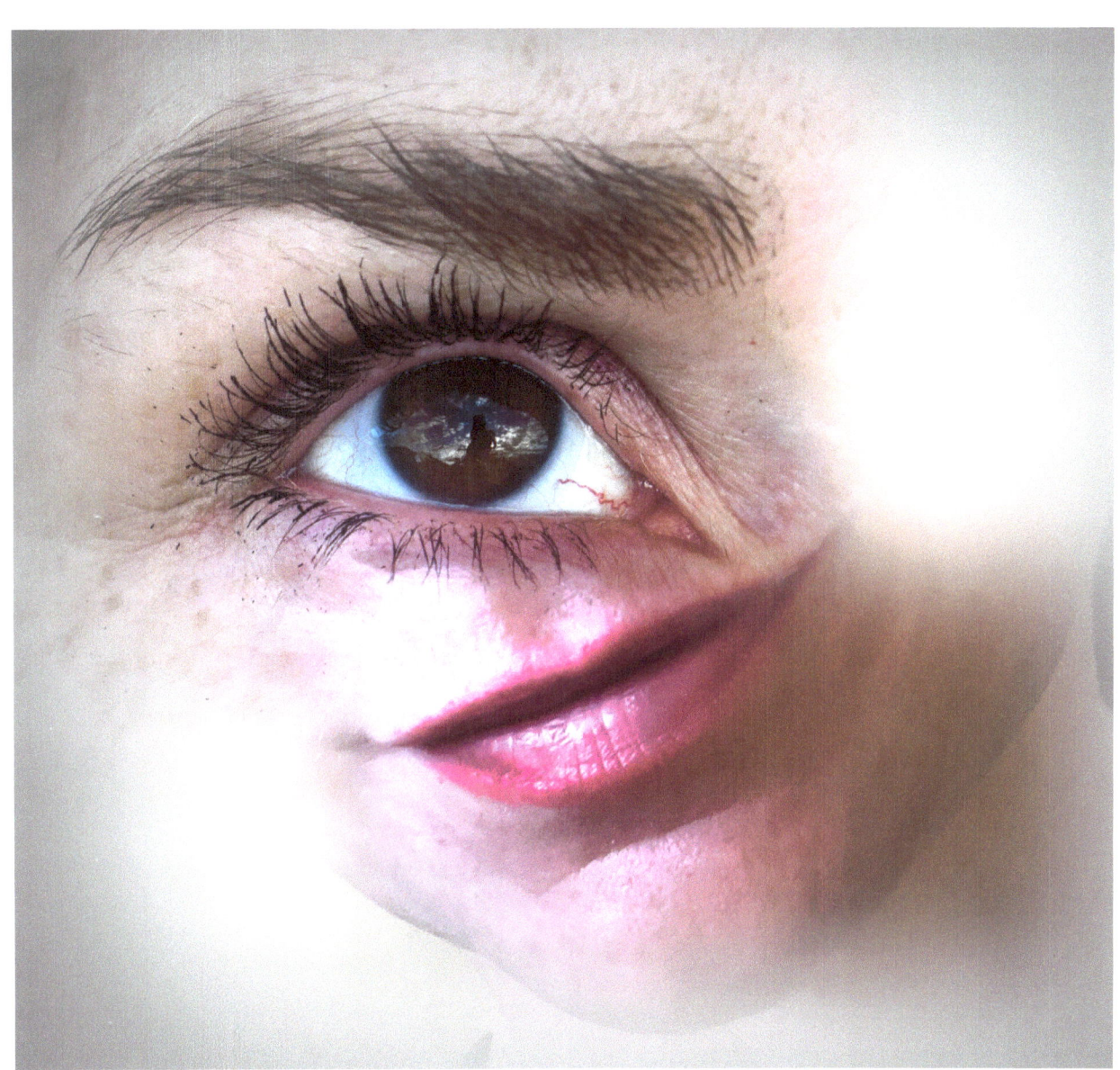

Brandon Soder

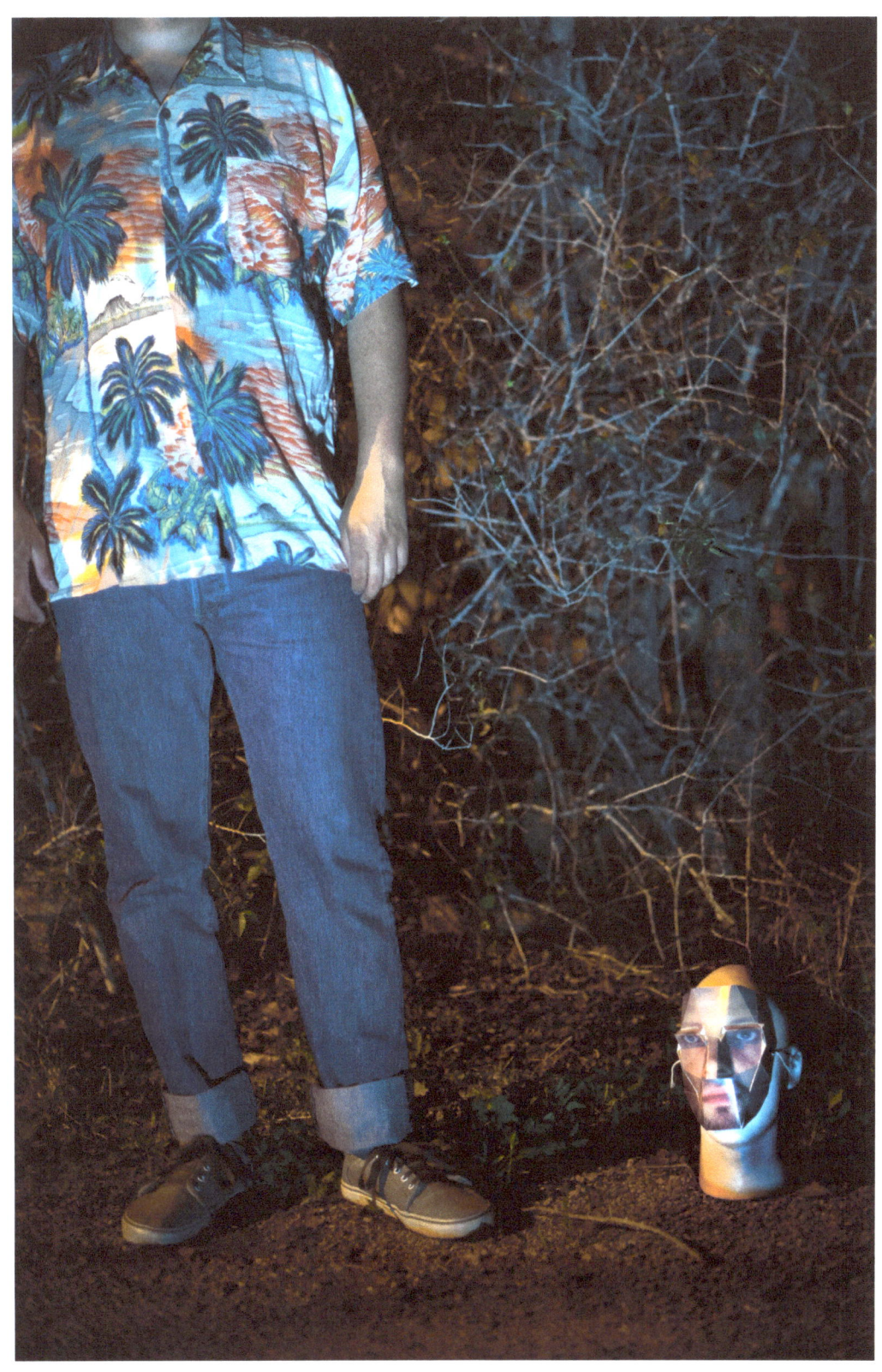

Catie Soldan

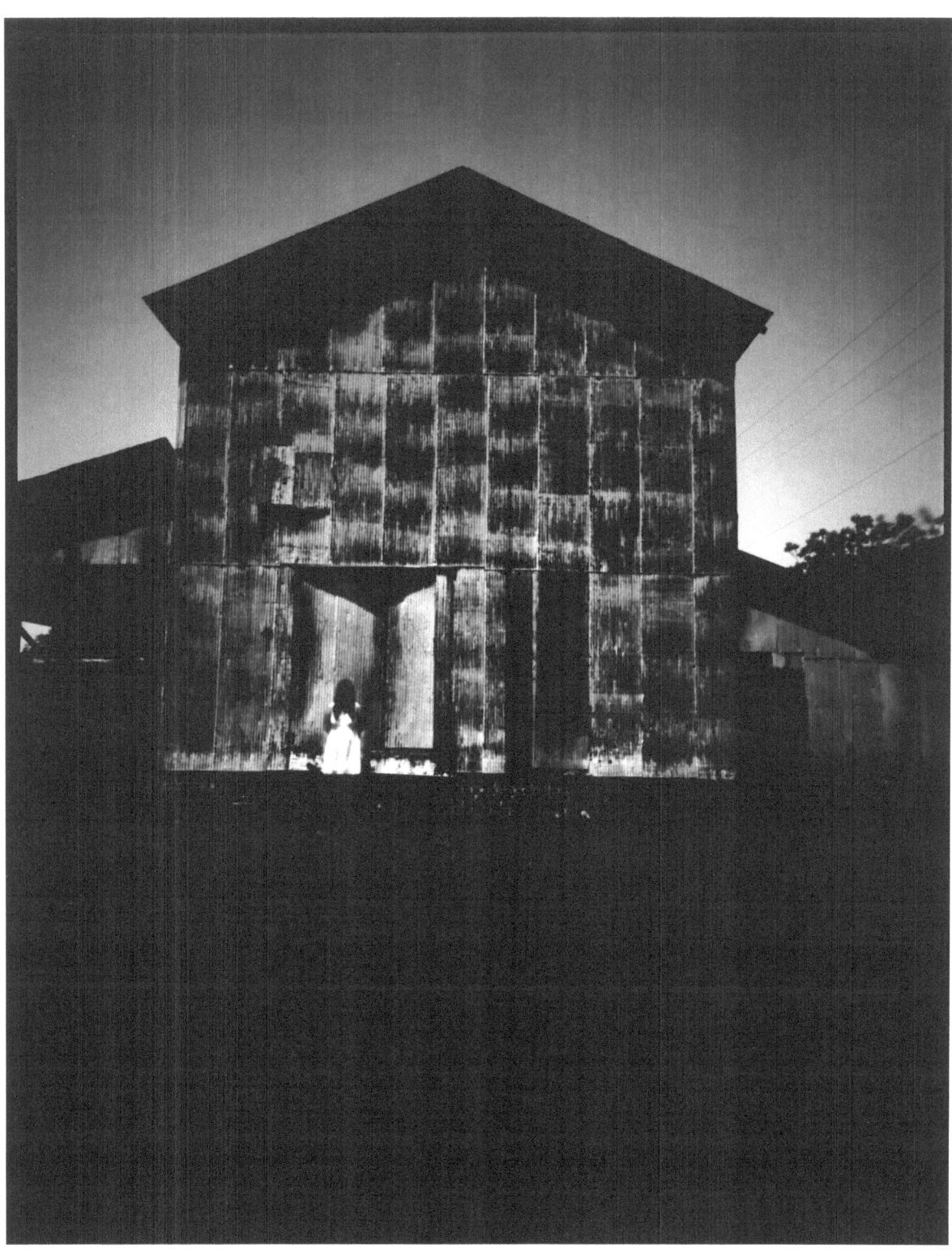

Nancy Sutor

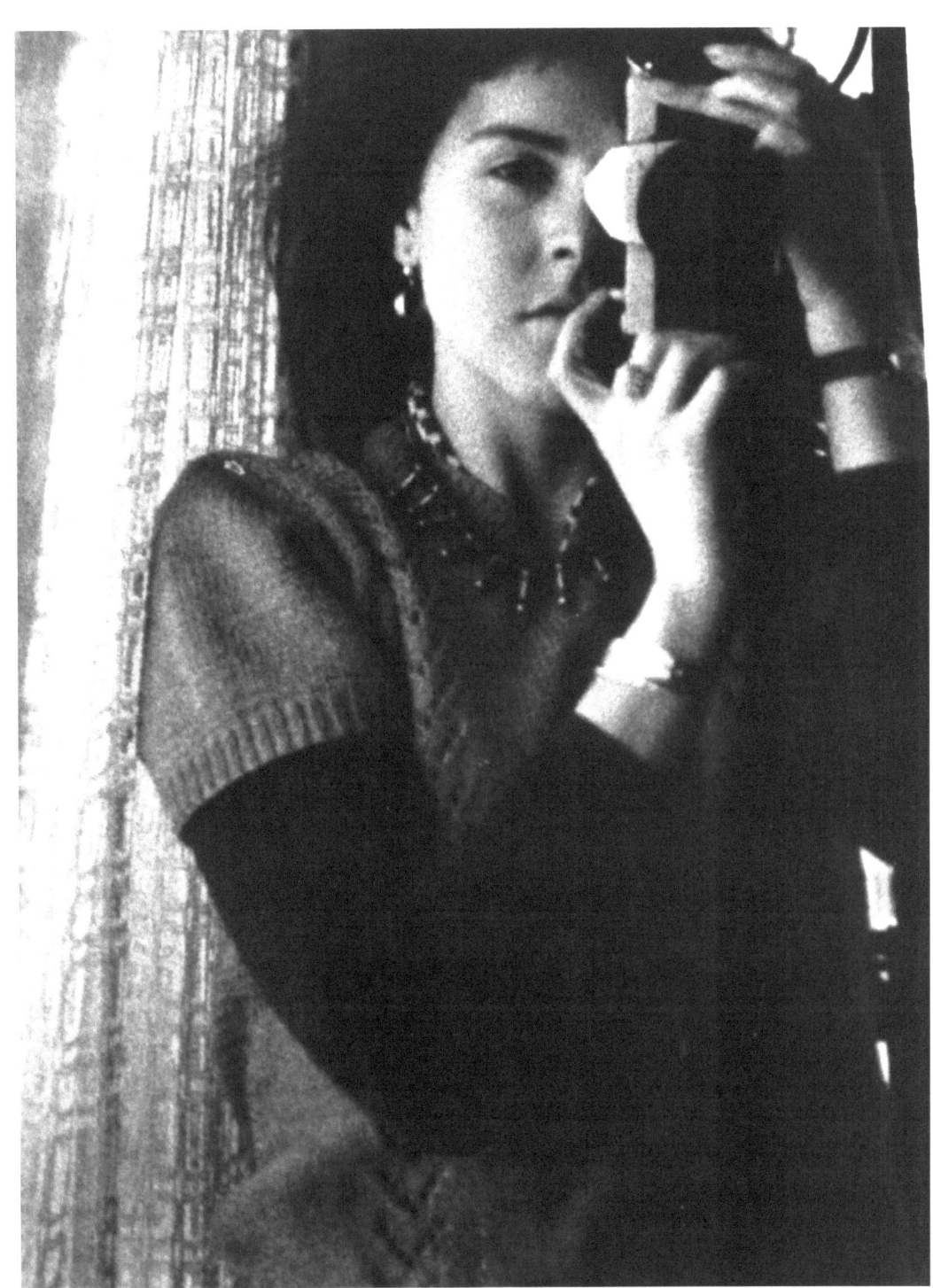

Anne Staveley

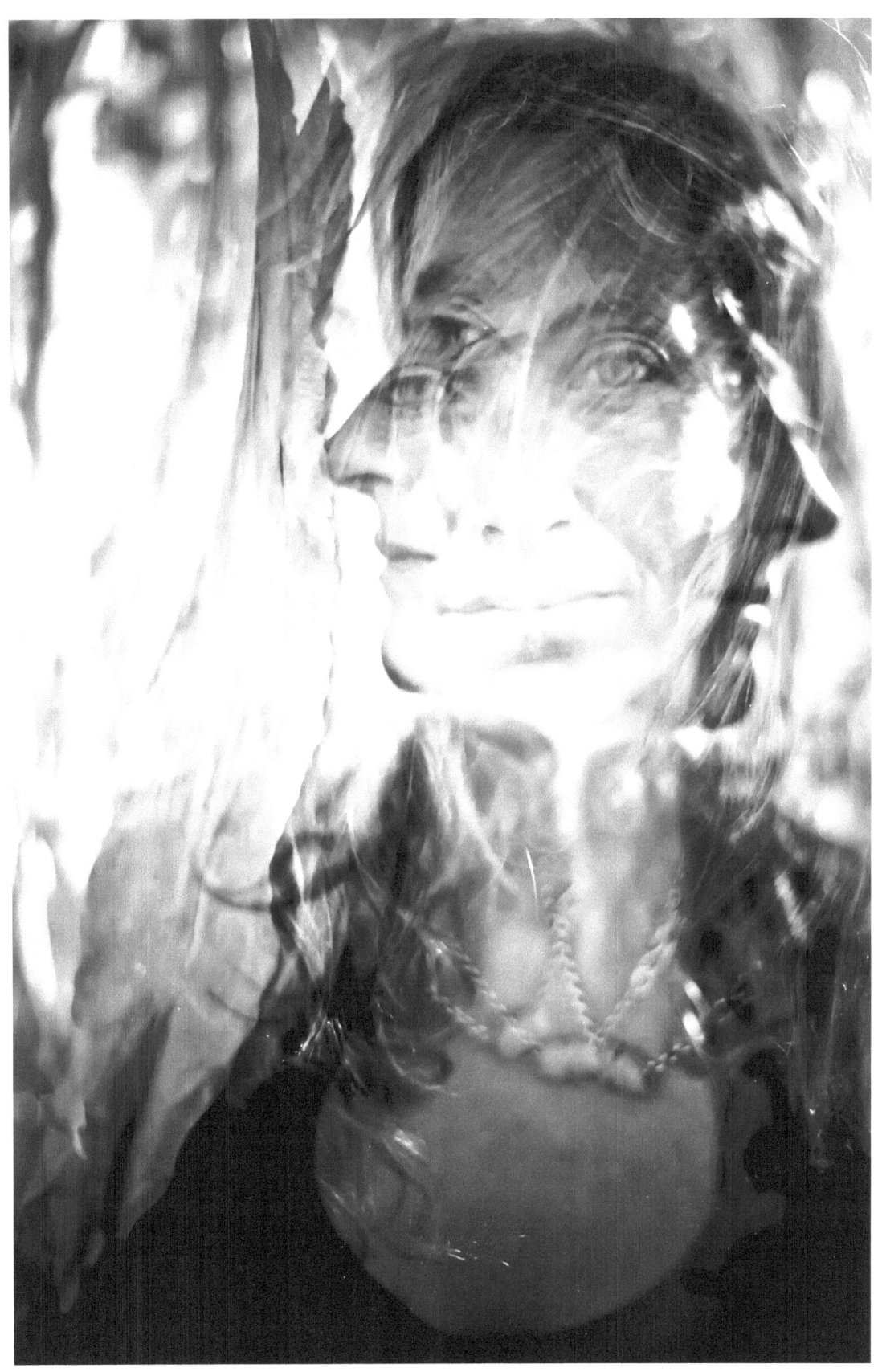

Sharon Stewart

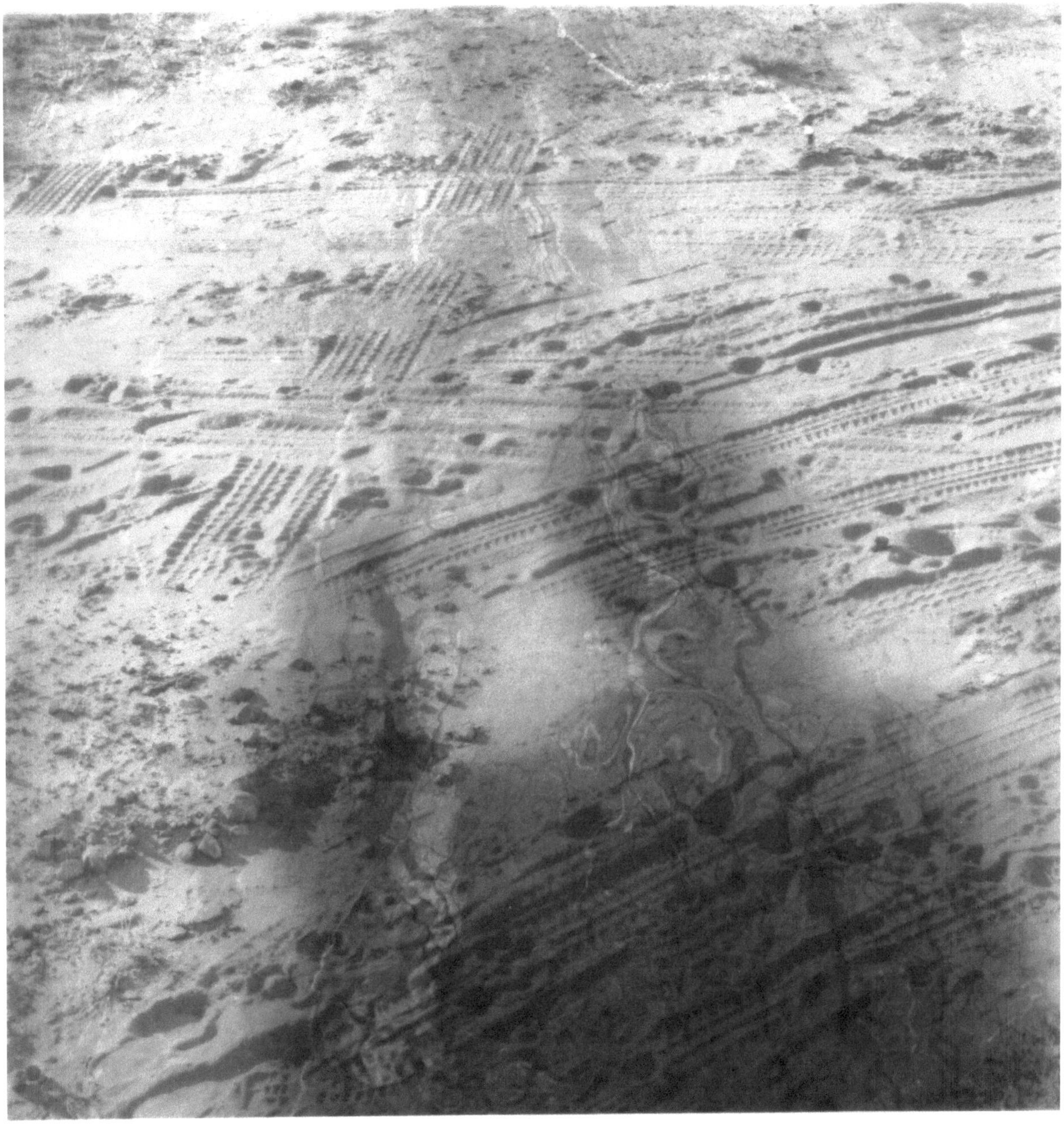

Jamey Stillings

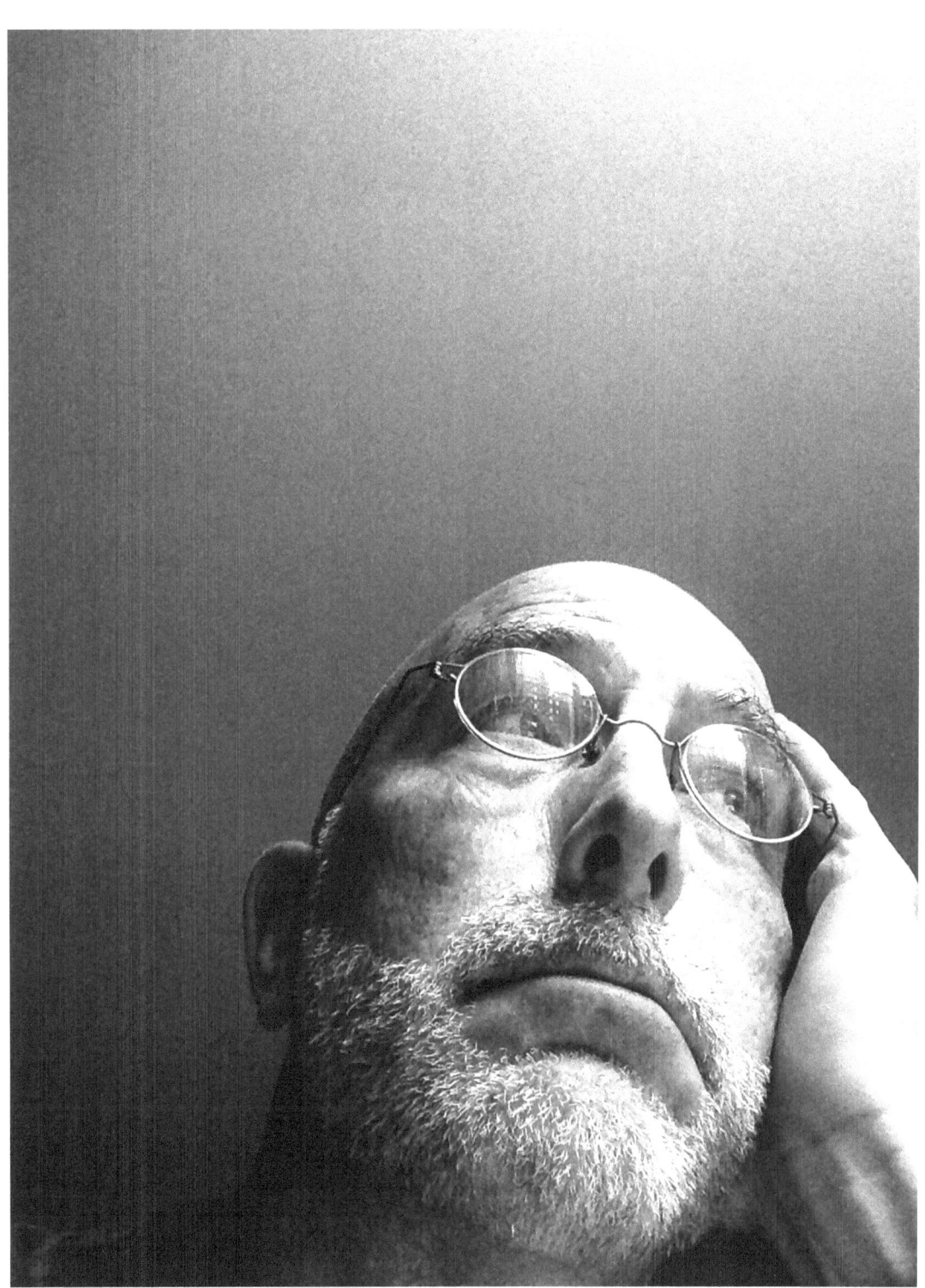

Robert Stivers

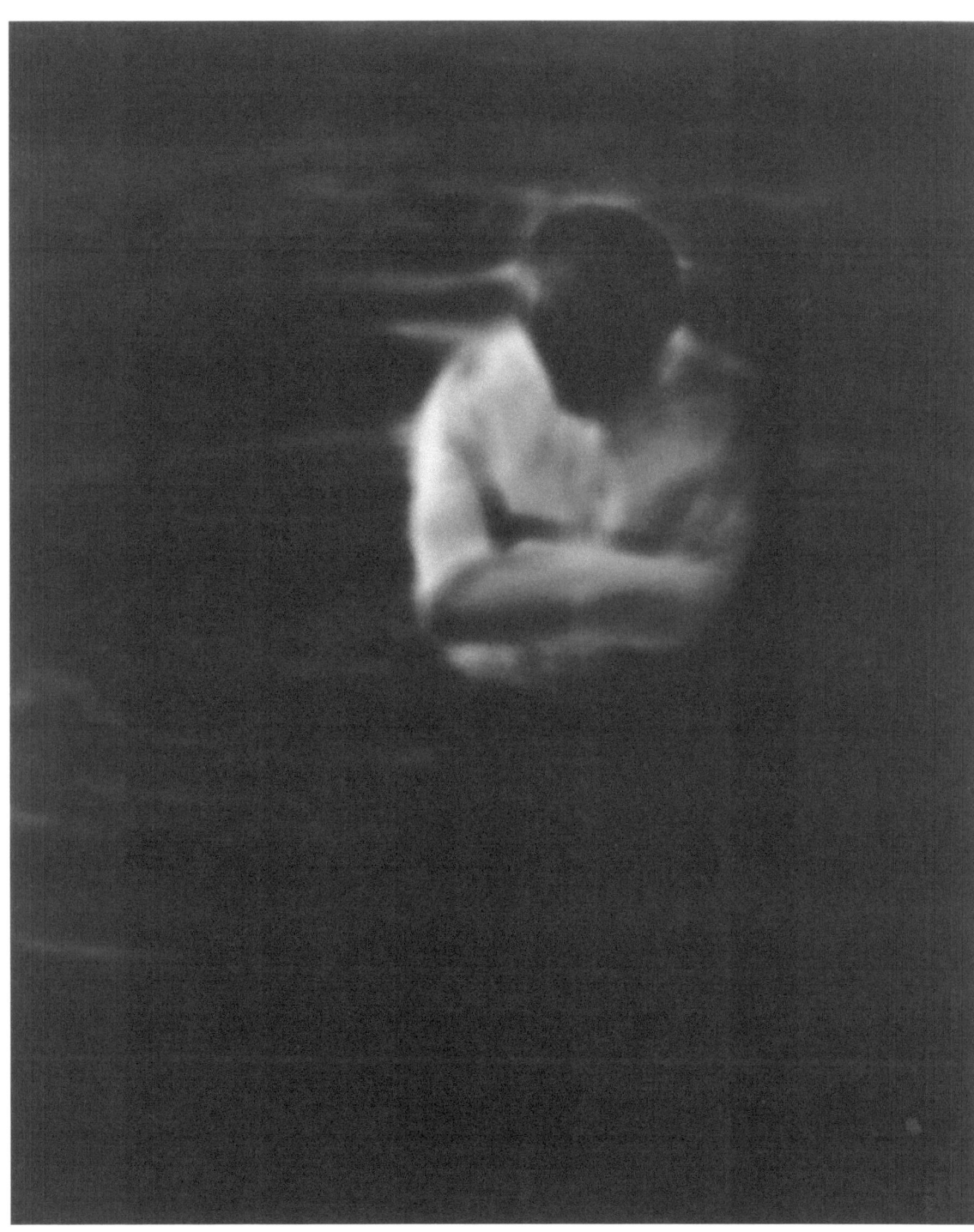

Dianne Stromberg

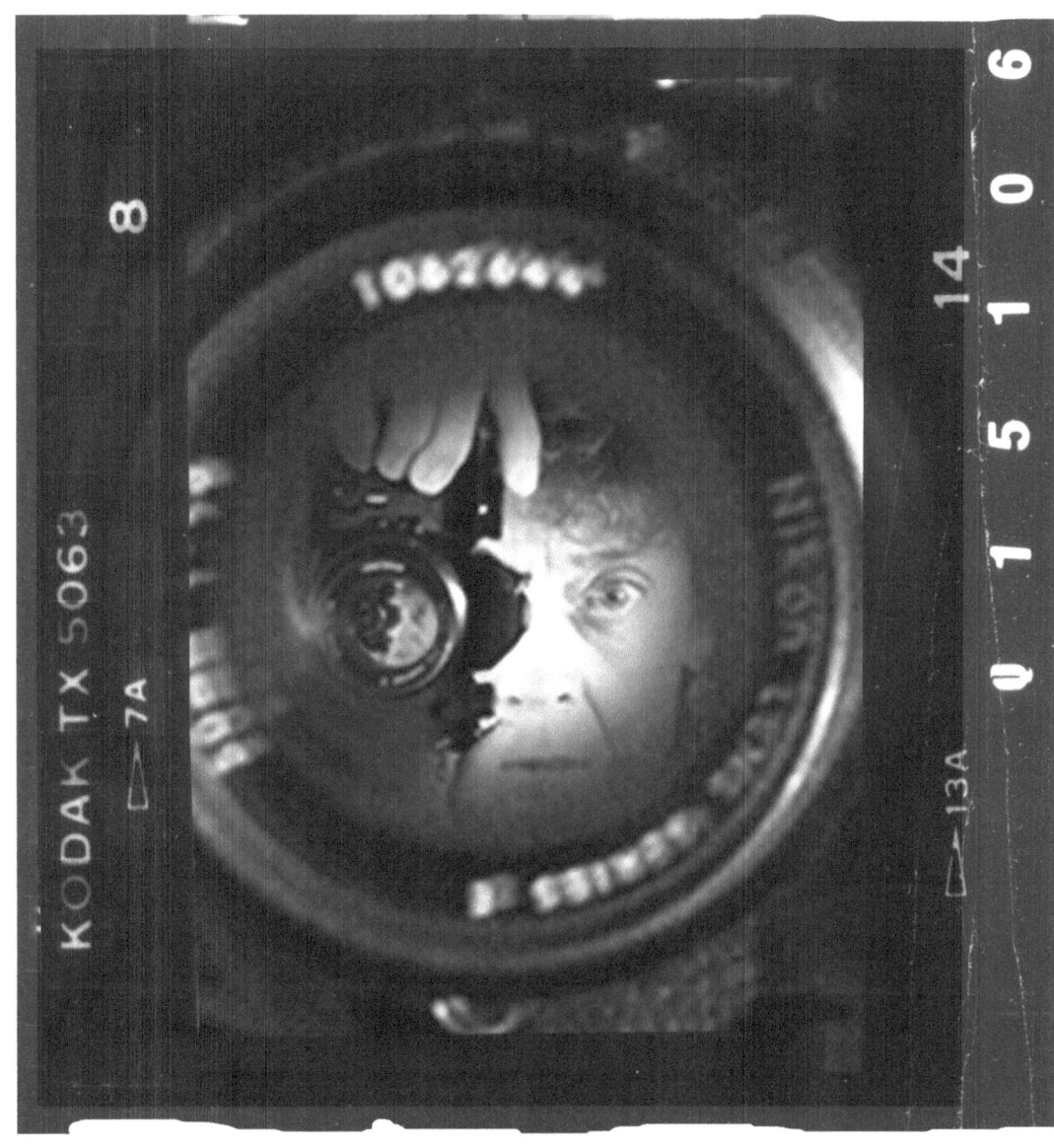

Jim Stone

An invitation arrived from a gallery to exhibit a self-portrait. I make
and exhibit portraits, but never turned the camera on myself seriously;
the practice of self-portraiture always seemed too narcissistic. It's not
politically correct but I found a homeless guy who looked like who I might
be when I get that old, and paid him twenty bucks to be photographed.

Martin Stupich

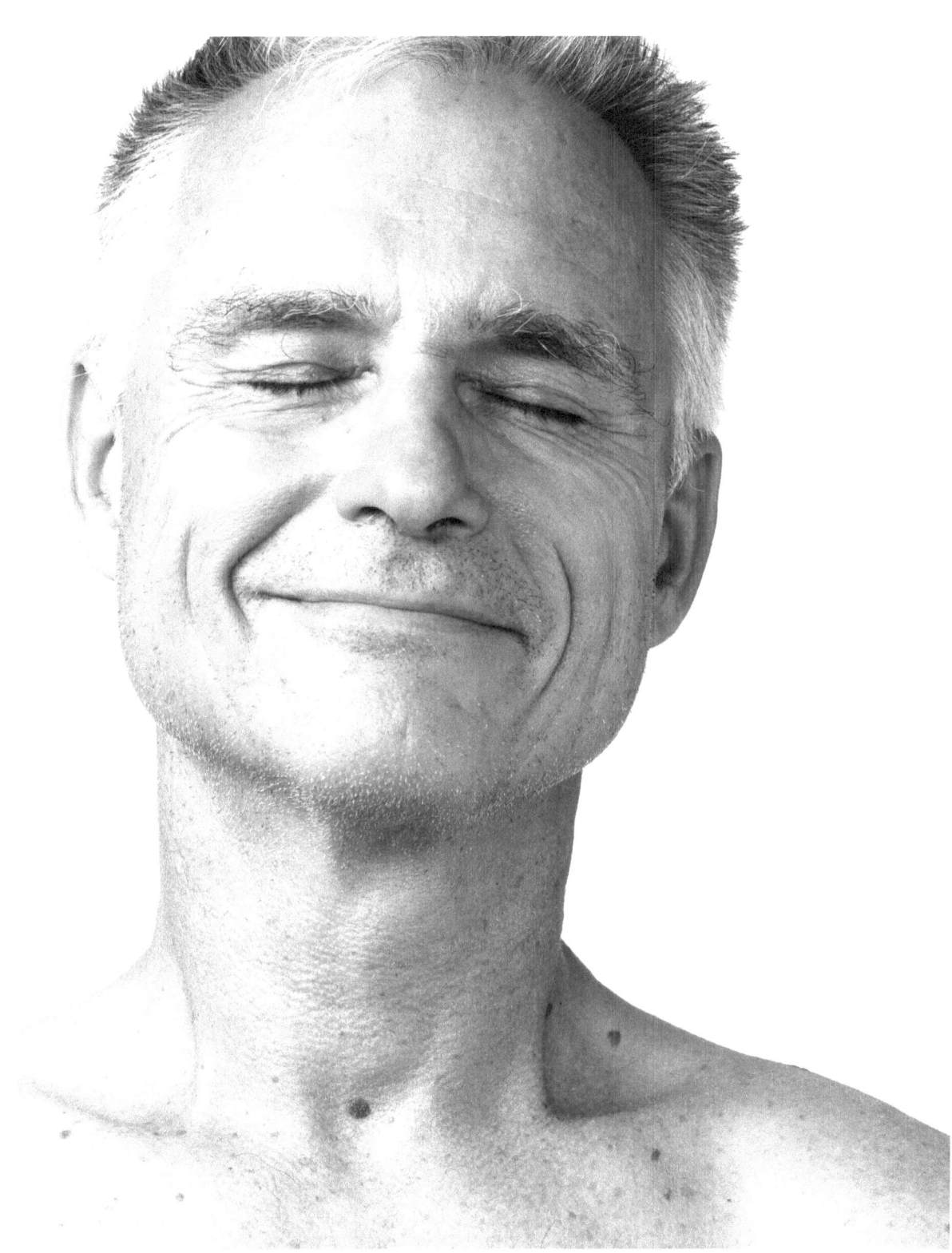

Carrie Tafoya

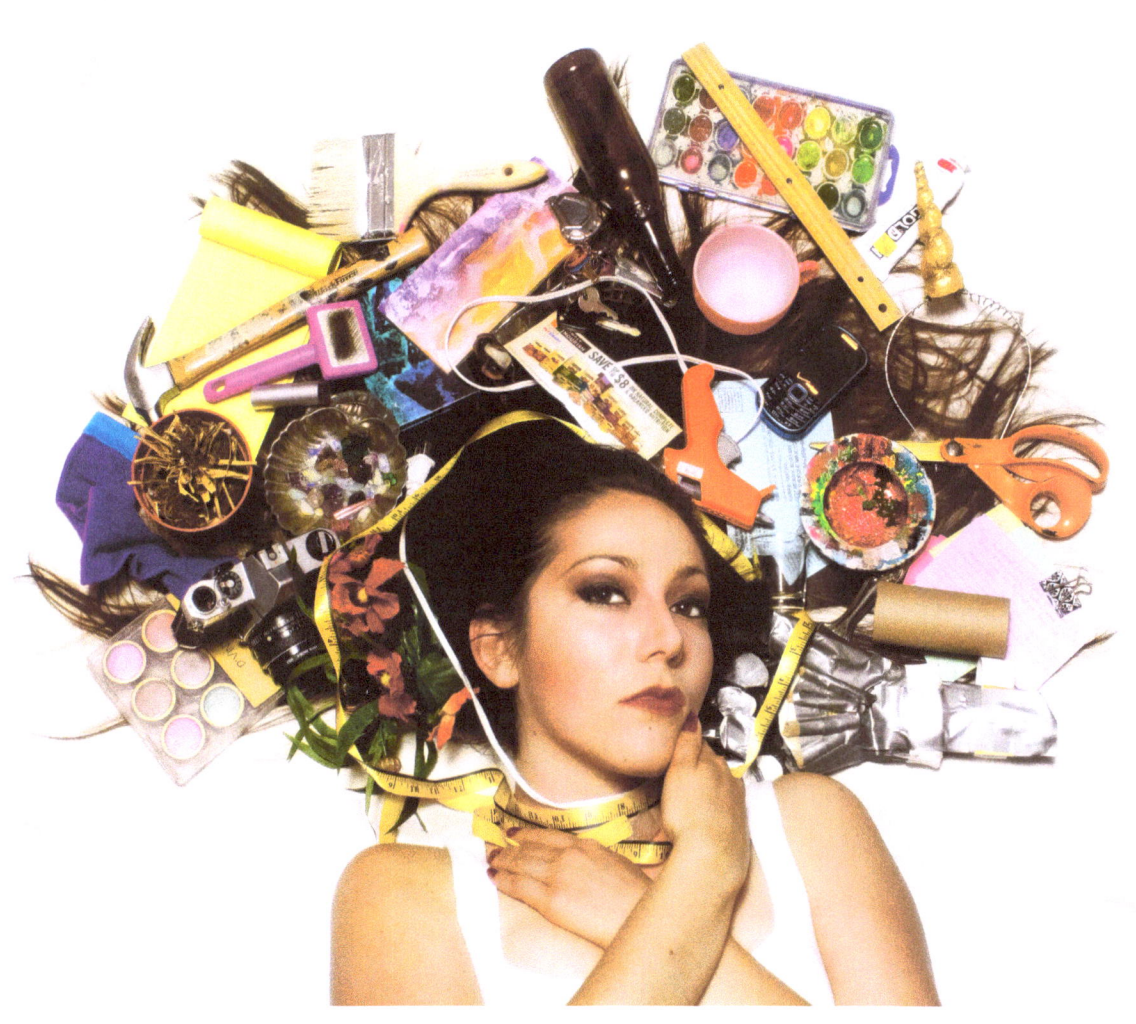

Laurie Tümer

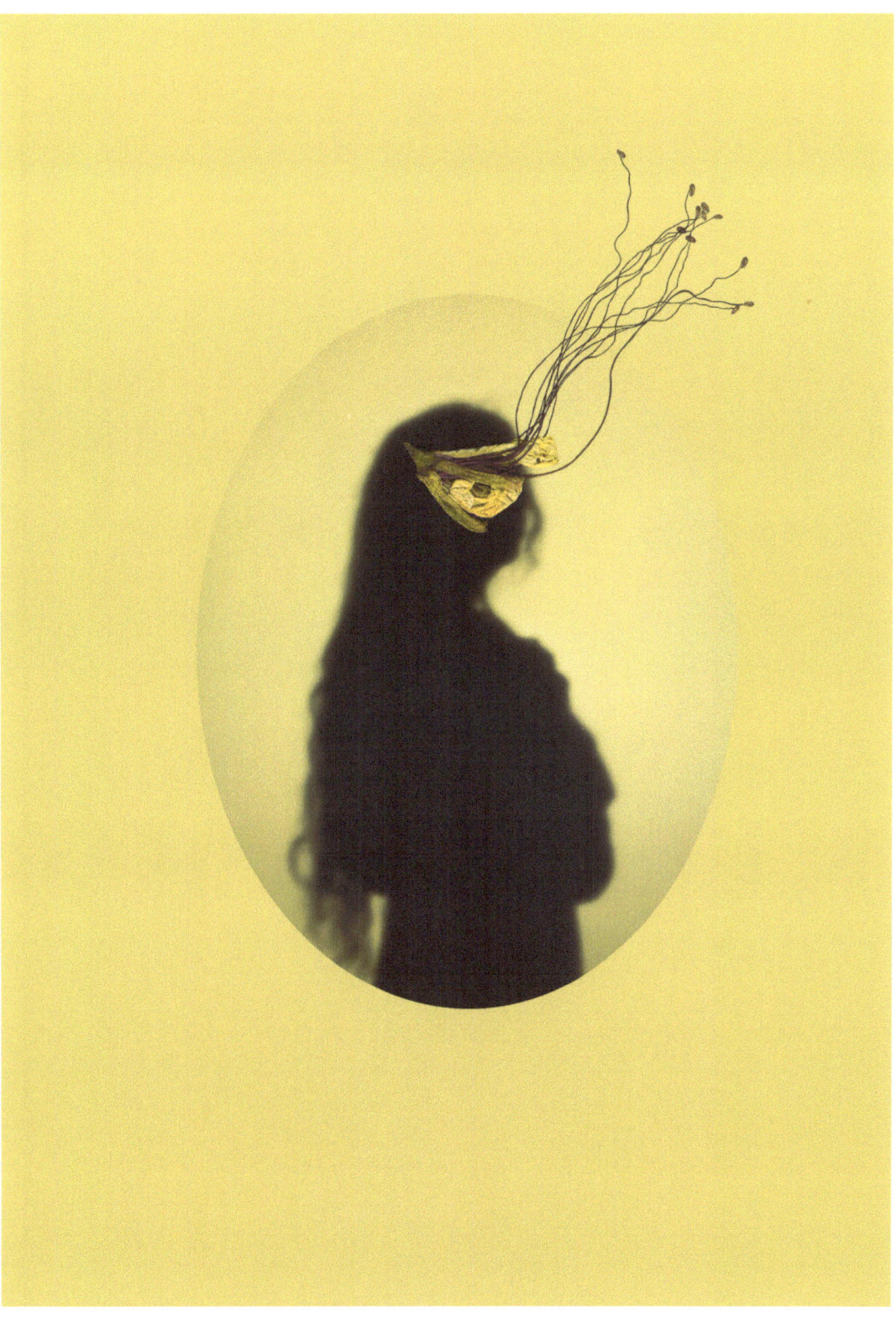

Lisa Tyrrell

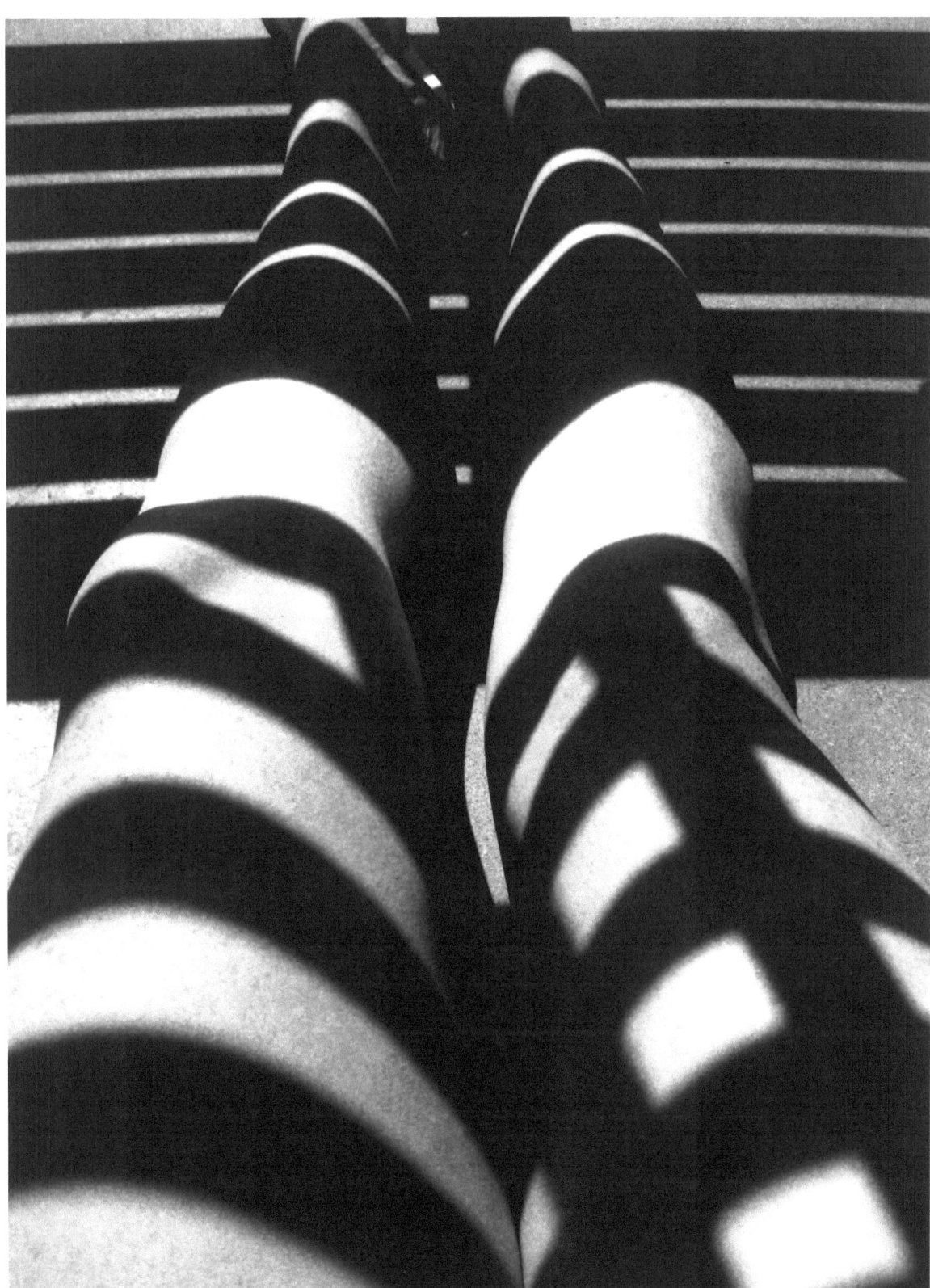

Marion Wasserman

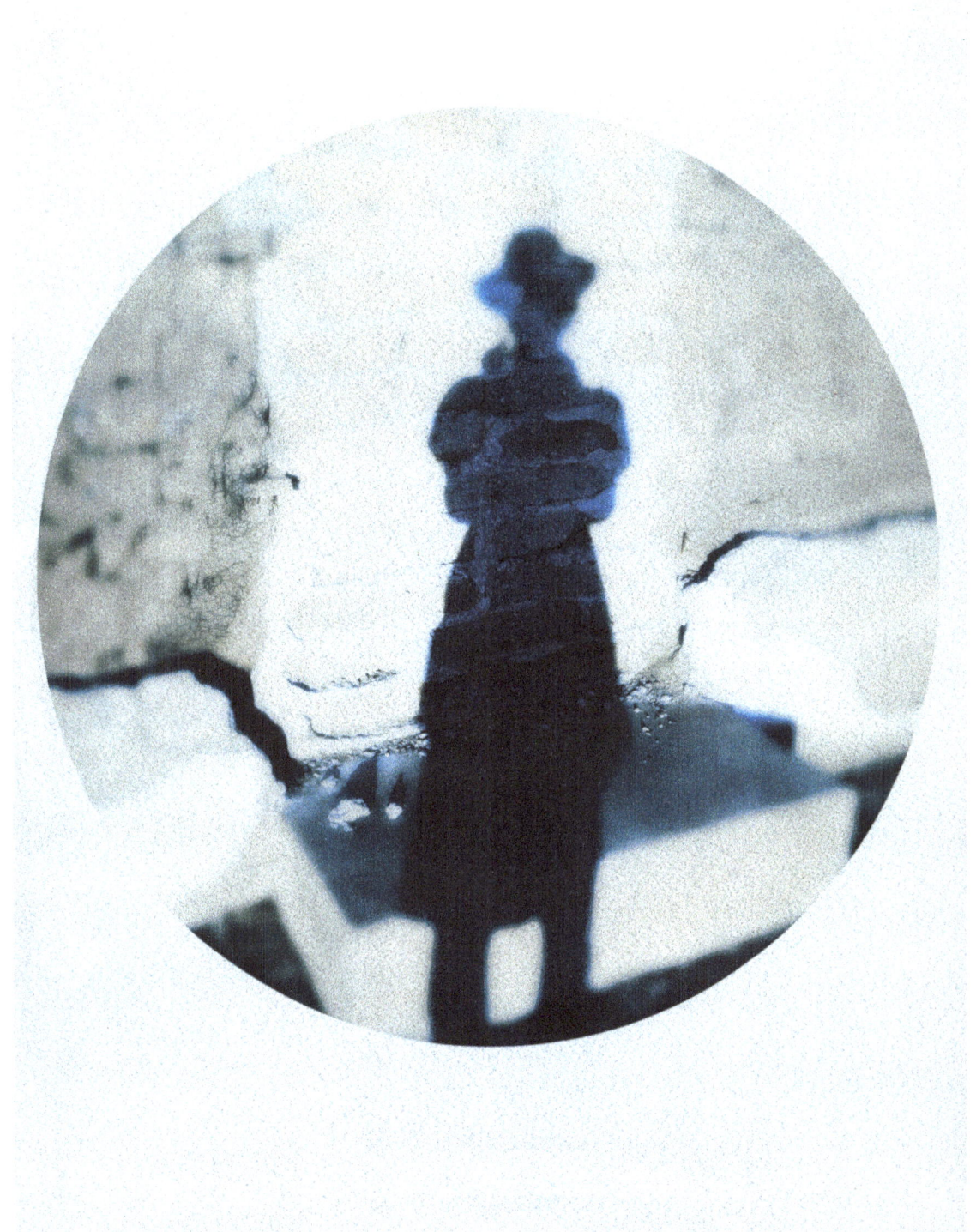

Melanie West

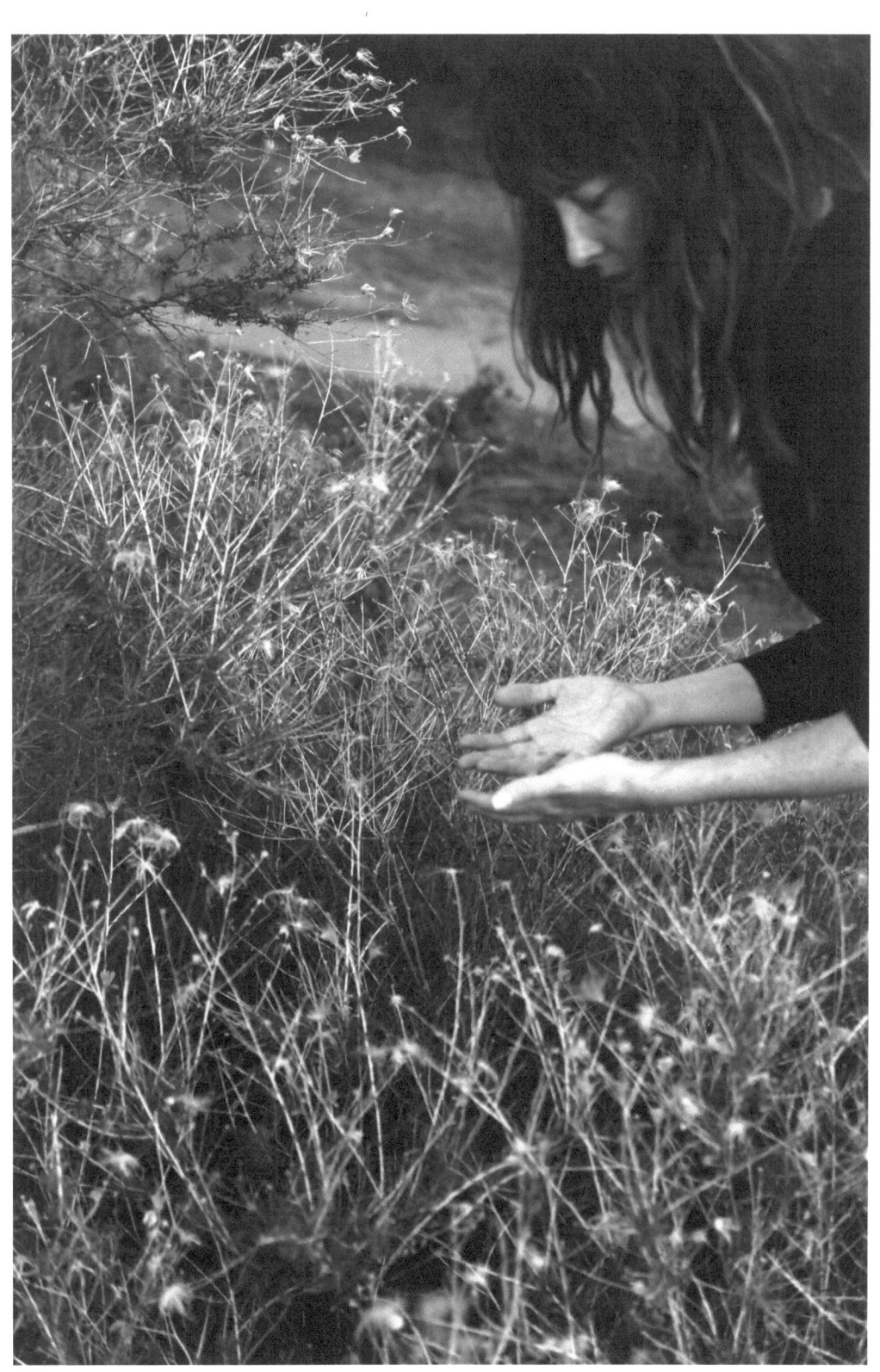

Will Wilson

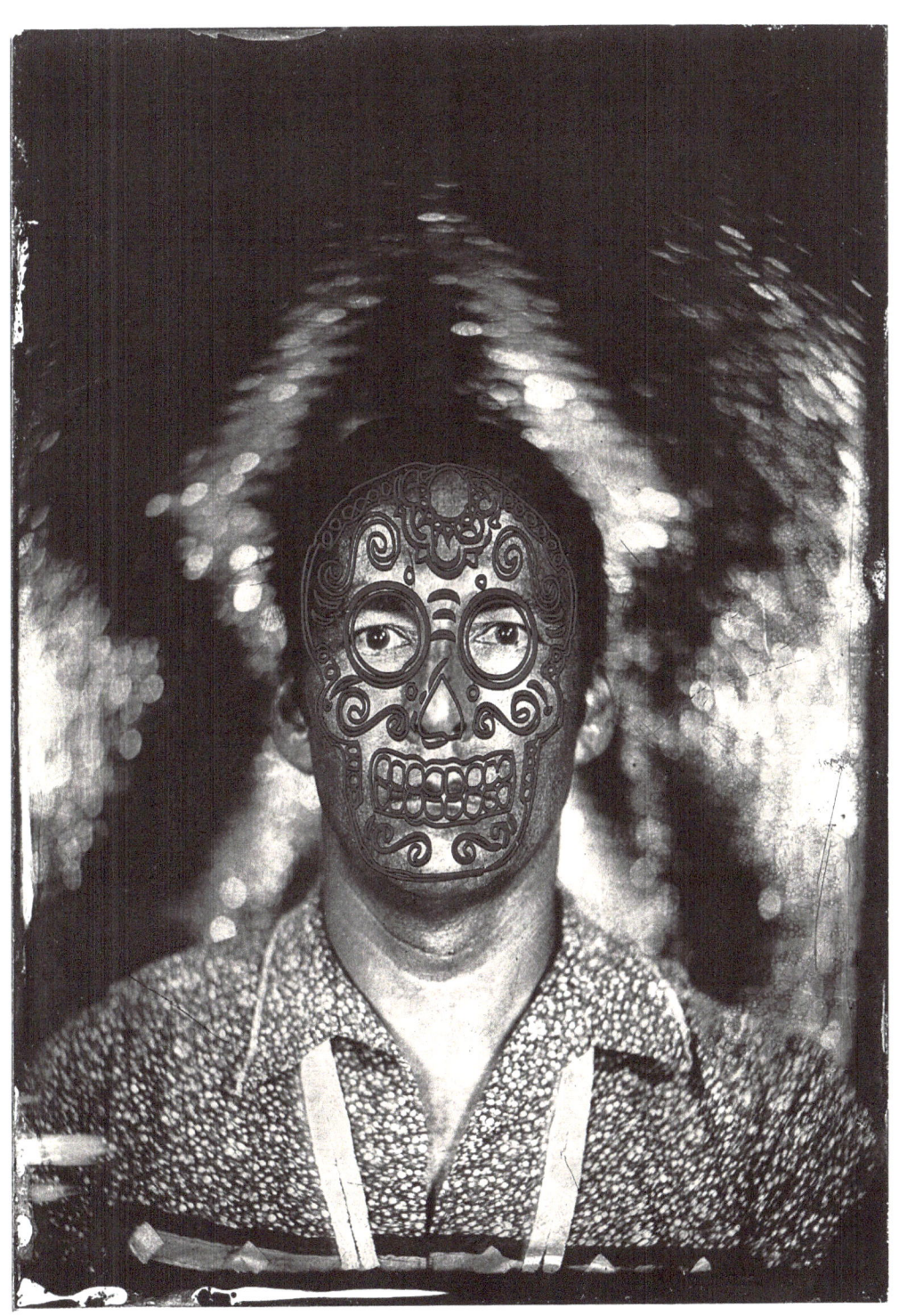

Baron Wolman

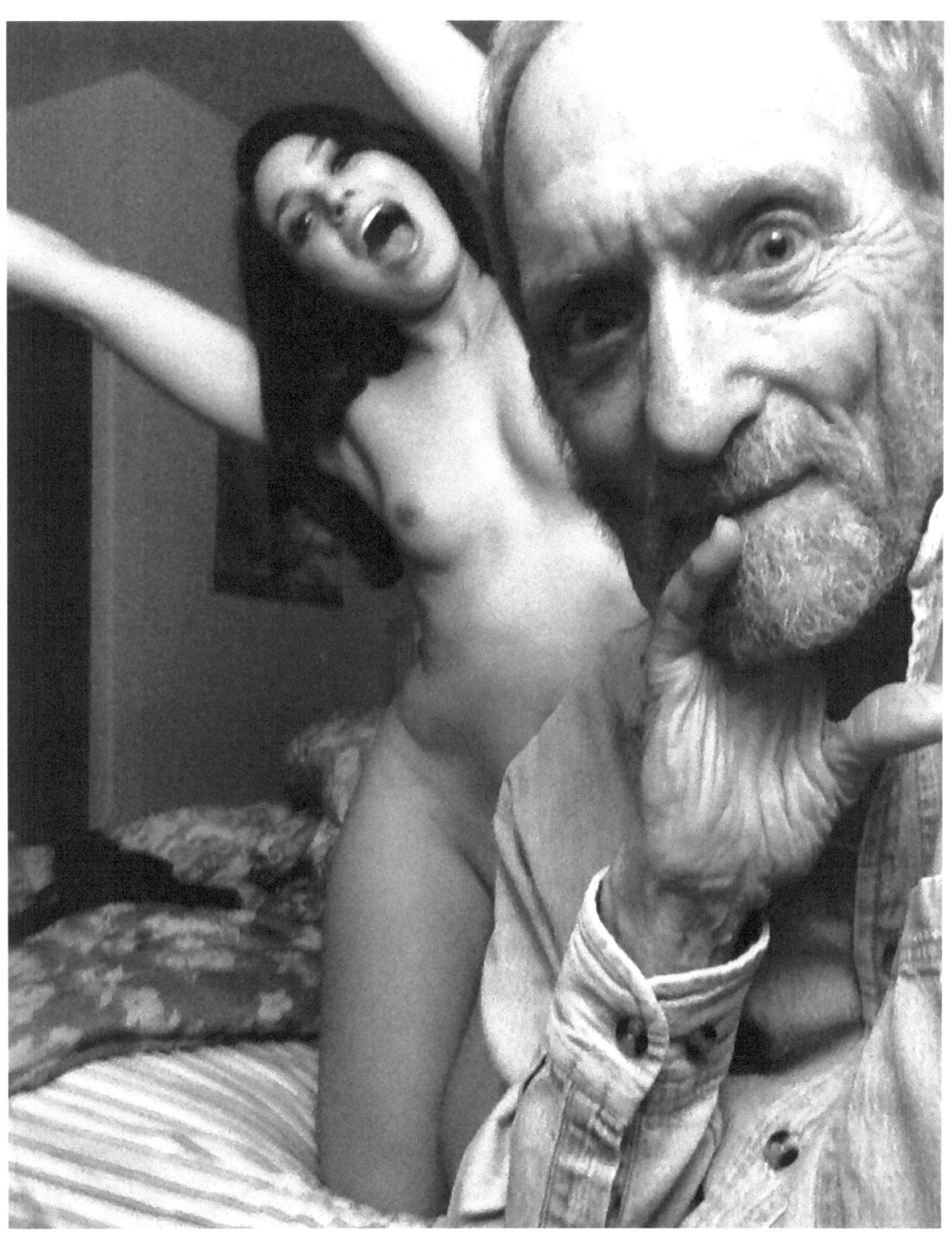

Francesca Yorke

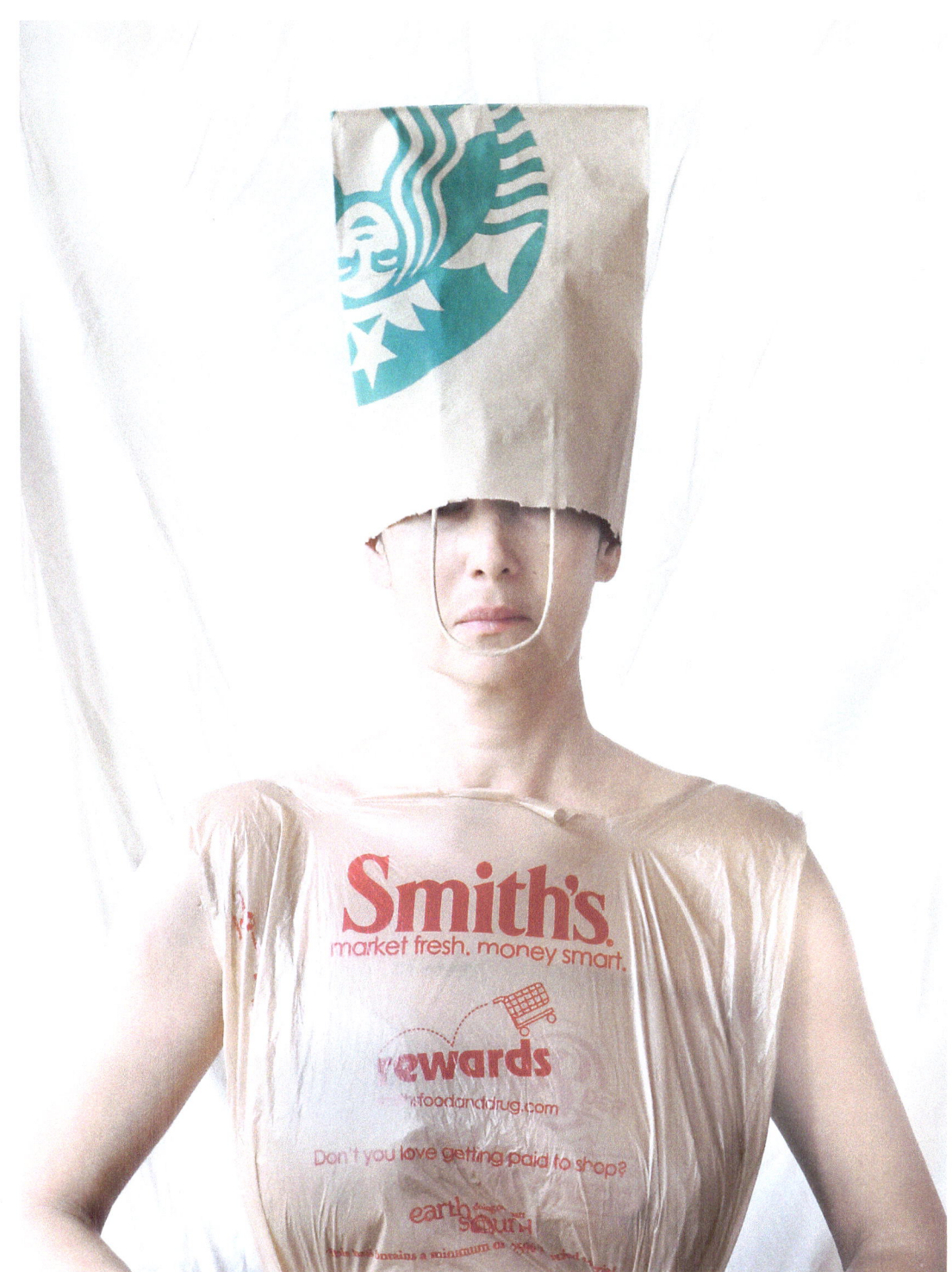

Joan Zalenski

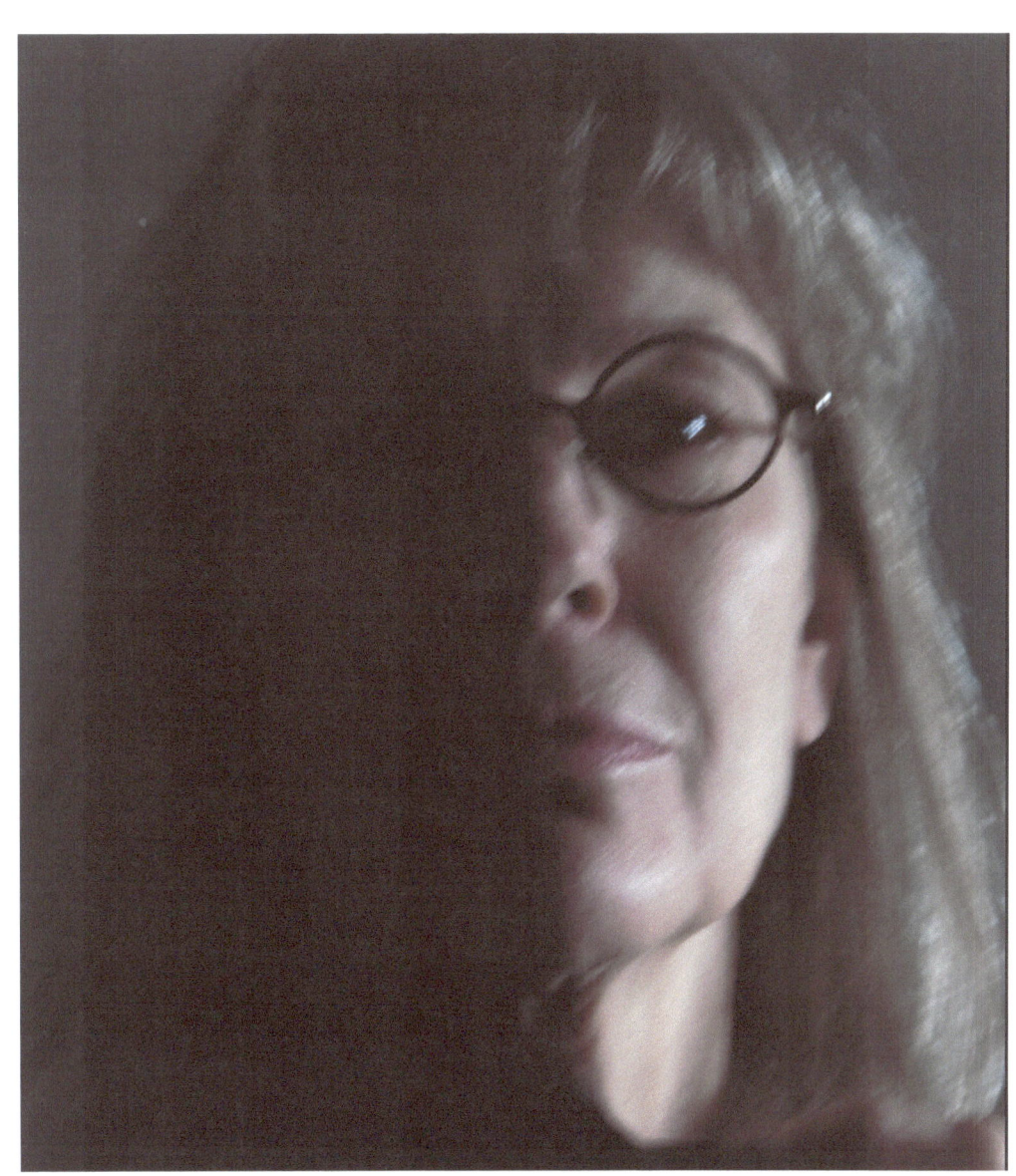

Zoë Zimmerman

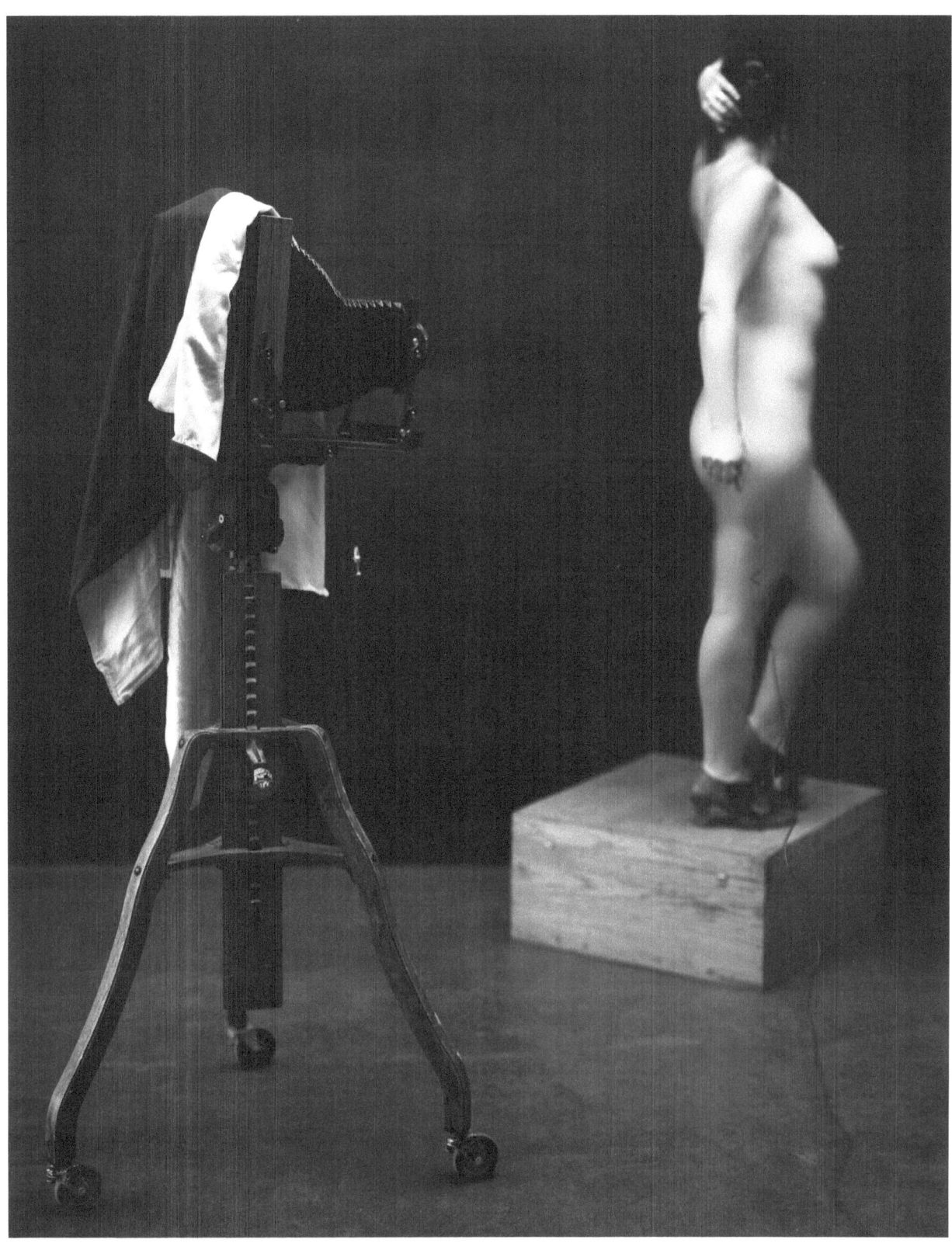

www.ingramcontent.com/pod-product-compliance
Lightning Source LLC
Chambersburg PA
CBHW050712180526
45159CB00003B/1010